"In a time where conversation is replaced with text messaging, and dinner equals Grubhub, there is still no place like home. As an entrepreneur running several businesses, a wife, mom, sister, and friend, life can get busy, and those conveniences make life seem a lot easier. Sometimes, in the hustle and bustle of it all, you need a gentle reminder of what's truly important. With every page and each photo of *Hungry for Home*, I felt like I was sharing a cool glass of lemonade on a warm summer day with the people I love most… my family. It thoughtfully transitions through the seasons with beautiful indoor/outdoor décor ideas, comforting meal recipes, and most importantly, traditions that can be shared with you and your family for years to come. I never thought all the beautiful feelings of home, family, and love could be encapsulated onto the pages of a book, but somehow she did it. And all roads lead to home!"

—**Terri Matthews, *author, Emmy award-winning television host, businesswoman, and autism-advocate***

"Ruth McKeaney's personal stories and wise words will spark readers to rethink and reimagine what home life can be! *Hungry For Home* shows how family traditions and recipes feed our souls. This book provides a roadmap to make moments at home both meaningful and memorable. Thank you, Ruth, for sharing your unique talents and insights—you've created a home filled with love and joy, and it's fun to feel inspired. Blessed indeed by *Hungry For Home*."

—**Sarah Perot, *President of the Sarah and Ross Perot, Jr. Foundation***

"You will experience a nostalgia for all things family and togetherness as you take in every page of *Hungry For Home*. I found myself not only getting inspired to try new recipes and introduce fun new traditions, but it caused me to hit the pause-button on the lightning-paced speed that life has become. Ruth has magically found a way to give practical and attainable ideas for this very busy mom to start incorporating into her home. It's a beautiful reminder that leaving a legacy of memories in the form of time spent together with your family at HOME is so much more important than anything money can buy."

—**Jill Donovan, *author, speaker, former attorney and law professor, and the founder of Rustic Cuff***

Hungry for Home

Hungry for Home

A Year Together at Hillside Farm

RUTH MCKEANEY

HfH

To Bob,

Wherever you are,
I'm home.

HILLSIDE
FARM

CONTENTS

A LETTER FROM RUTH

"Home is the nicest word there is."
Laura Ingalls

My husband and I own a charming historic home, Hillside Farm, just outside of Philadelphia. It's a lovely property with giant trees and rolling hills, an enormous barn, a chicken coup, and a constant stream of friends and family.

At Hillside, my days are spent shuttling my kids back and forth from swim meets and school trips, baking for the next visitor, and working in my garden. It is a busy, full life that Bob and I have come to cherish.

The thought of writing about our life at Hillside never occurred to me. Rather, the idea for this book was planted during a lunch with friends. "Ruth," they said adamantly, "you have to write about this!"

"This?" I asked curiously.

"The farm! Your story! Your life."

Really? Write about my life at Hillside? I chuckled and put the idea in my back pocket, never expecting to take it out again. But, like a persistent seed, the idea refused to stay buried. Instead, it took root and sprouted straight up. And before I knew it, one page after another, a book was born. It took all of us working together. My daughters did the calligraphy and illustrations, and Bob cheered me on.

Like Hillside, the book is a representation of Bob and me. We have restored many fixer-uppers to their former glory, but Hillside is the apex of our rehab adventures. For one year, we documented our life at the farm. From our favorite traditions and time-earned wisdom, to family recipes, gardening ideas, and hosting tips, we captured what "home" means to us. It is our hope that you will feel at home in its pages and be encouraged to make your house a home for others as well.

Welcome to Hillside Farm.

Love,
Ruth M.

COMING
HOME

People are born with an innate desire to belong.

WE are designed to grow roots, to know the love of a parent, to enjoy the pleasure of shared secrets with siblings, to trust our tribe.

HOME is the foundation for a full, abundant life. One where we share burdens, embrace frailty, and encourage greatness.

HOME is where we mourn with those who mourn and rejoice with those who rejoice.

HOME is how we welcome others and love truly.

HOME chooses peace, truth, goodness, and hardwork over the easy way out.

WE are all hungry for home in a world where homemaking is quickly becoming a lost art.

BUT it's not lost yet. Restoration is always possible. Great things can grow out of ruins. Families can thrive in places once unfit for life. Demolish the rot and rebuild your walls. Start on a new foundation if necessary.

TAKE it from me, you will never regret the effort it takes to make your house a *HOME*.

Our Story

Way back in 1997, Bob's roommate hosted a party… and I happened to go to it. At the time, I was an Assistant Attorney General, and Bob was in sales. We're a case of opposites attracting. I'm low-risk, serious, and a "big picture" sort of person. Bob is risky, makes the most mundane exercise fun, and is detail-oriented. He's also the hardest worker I've ever met. On our first date, he wouldn't even come inside my apartment until he'd fixed the screen door.

That's Bob. When he sees something that needs to be done, he does it. It's one of the reasons I love him.

Just after we married, about a year and a half after that first date, we made our first foray into the realm of rehab. Bob's bachelor house desperately needed new cabinets, and, obviously, new cabinets necessitated a new floor.

How hard could it be to put in new tile? We confidently ripped out the old linoleum, mixed up some mortar, and spread it all over a floor covered in plywood. Time for a break before laying our tile!

It was just for a quick dinner. Certainly, nothing could go wrong!

Well, if you know anything about mortar and plywood, you know that something did go wrong. We came back to a kitchen of rock-hard mortar on plywood that had to be chiseled up piece by piece before we could start all over and get back to business.

Bob and I still laugh about it.

After he realized what had happened, he politely asked me to leave the house so he could lose his temper in private—a move that served us well time and time again in our learning how to renovate homes.

Following our first project, Bob went to work for his family's business. This required moving from Richmond, Virginia to Philadelphia, which was easy for Bob but incredibly difficult for me, not just because of a drastic change in my career, but because it meant leaving my family shortly after learning my mom had cancer.

But we still thought it was all going to work out smoothly, and that just wasn't the case. Bob's new job didn't pay enough for a new home, and I was jobless, waiting to waive into the bar in PA. Couple that with Bob's bachelor house not selling and learning I was pregnant! We wound up staying with nine different families that year in various basements and guest-rooms, living out of our luggage like nomads.

From One House to Another

Two years later, we had enough in savings to put a down payment on a house in Pennsylvania, a150-year-old home sliding off its foundation. When our realtor showed us the house (the only thing we could afford in the area), I burst into tears, but Bob was undaunted. Never mind that the entire thing had to be redone. Never mind that we would have no money left to hire contractors to fix it. And never mind that we had two babies under 18 months. Bob said let's go to Home Depot and learn.

And so began a decade and a half of flipping houses every 18 to 24 months, moving around almost constantly. All the while, we were expanding our family to 7. Each of our 5 kids was born in a different house.

Honestly, restoring homes was never something Bob and I saw ourselves doing. Bob is a salesman, and I'm a lawyer who dreamed of one day being a judge. But "necessity is the mother of invention," as the saying goes. And in those days, Bob and I were doing a lot of inventing. Thankfully, what we were doing was beginning to work. We tackled one troubled property, only to take on an even more difficult project a year later.

And so, a partnership was born. Bob's get-it-done, fun approach to life merged with my visionary, serious steadiness.

As a team, we possessed the unique gift of restoration. We saw what could be instead of what was. We discovered that mistakes can be corrected, wiring replaced, small spaces enlarged, and old homes once discarded could be made habitable. More than habitable, really. We could make them comfortable, beautiful, charming... a home.

The process was always the same. We'd find an old house with character and scrape together enough for a down payment. I'd gather inspiration from magazines and books by designers and architects I liked. Trusted friends with good design sense would volunteer their services for complex spaces.

At this time, I still didn't have much experience with artistry. Homemaking and cooking were foreign fields. Just choosing a paint color for a kitchen was a stretching experience. I had to learn a whole new set of skills, and I had to learn them quickly.

Before starting, Bob and I would go out for coffee with a notebook and write out our "wish list" and our "no compromise list" in order to make sure we were on the same page before diving into the rehab. With that, we were off to the races.

At Home at Hillside Farm

History of Hillside

We raised our family amidst power tools and architectural plans.

Alexandra, Avery, AnnaScott, Audrey, and Anders joined the tribe and, as of this writing, range in age from 11-20. They love to help us on our projects and can often be seen with power tools in hand.

That said, while we all became comfortable with rehab and moving every other year, as the kids grew older, the need for something more permanent grew as well. This fact became all the more apparent in 2007 after my mother passed away. We needed a solid foundation, a house to call home. Bob and I are two of the most dedicated homebodies on the planet. It was time to find a place to lay the tools aside for a while and grow roots in our own backyard—with no plans to move again in the near future.

My dream property was one with a guest house for my father to stay in whenever he wanted and a big yard for the kids to run around. But… our budget was moderate. I couldn't imagine being able to afford the kind of property I desired. Then my dear friend Heather and her husband told us they had "found our house." They'd visited Hillside Farm as prospective buyers themselves, but the minute they stepped foot on the property, they saw us living there. It had not just one guest house but two. And this wasn't just a house with a big backyard. Nope. It was a full-on farm. There were acres of land and a barn. Or at least, what was left of a barn. Truth be told, the main house and most of the outbuildings were completely uninhabitable.

Regardless, Bob and I both knew it the moment we saw it. Despite the ruins, the dust, and the weeds, aside from the archaic plumbing, the rotting wood, the trees growing into the third floor, and a roof with holes so large the sun shone through, Hillside Farm was our home.

Within a matter of weeks, the sale closed, and the work of making our home began.

photos of hillside, 1914

CHARLES T. OKIE
ARCHITECT
DEVON, PENNSYLVANIA

Hillside began as a 300-acre dairy farm in 1717.

Nearly 200 years later, it underwent its first major restoration.

In 1902, Richardson Brognard Okie, who was then still a young, untried architect, managed to buy the old farm for $15,000. (The original deed to the property was signed over by William Penn.)

The house, a typical six-room tenant farmhouse, became Okie's architectural laboratory and a home for his wife and two children. The enormous barn sheltered his horses, who participated in the nearby Devon Horse Show, and his small herd of dairy cows. For over forty years, he made the long commute from his beloved farm into Philadelphia to work with his wealthy clientele until his untimely death in 1945.

Okie's Hillside

Okie's farm was a 90-acre plot that merged city and country, sophistication and rural practicality. Unlike many of the Colonial Revival homes Okie would later become famous for, Hillside retained its original personality and character.

The complementary relationship between the home and the landscape, the stylized farmstead, the undressed stone, and obsessive attention to detail—it's all Okie, and simultaneously, all Hillside.

Like many of the buildings Okie refurbished, it was difficult to separate what was his design and what was the original farmhouse.

As an architect, Okie was concerned with preserving historic details while introducing modern amenities. Of course, by the time we purchased the property, everything "modern" added by Okie was obsolete or completely unusable. The chandelier in the main house still had wax candles in it rather than electric lights!

Left: The Guesthouses of Hillside

The old playhouse was built at the turn of the twentieth century. It has a working stone fireplace and a beautiful brick floor. When we moved in, it was already wired for electricity. When they were little, the children spent hours inside playing "school" and "house."

The Ruins at Hillside

In the six decades following the esteemed architect's death, the home fell into complete disrepair. Due to arson, the barn had burned down, and many of the outbuildings were essentially ruins. Hillside was no longer the proud farmstead of Pennsylvania and Northern Delaware's quintessential architect. Rather, it was a sad memory of happier times gone past.

Work in progress...

It took over a year to renovate the home and the outbuildings enough to become livable. The old copper pipes were corroded to such an extreme that during our first week or two in the home, I flushed a toilet upstairs, and my husband (downstairs) was surprised by a gush of water that came down on his head like a waterfall.

I'll never forget standing in the basement with our beloved friend and architectural renderer, Betsy Grace, a local Okie expert, and discovering the original ax markings on the beams from 1717.

There are other lovely reminders of the past on the property. The original spring house from the dairy still works. I love to imagine the pots of cream and butter stored in the moss-covered stone-and-wood structure, a gentle stream running right through the middle. Then there is the old chicken coup built onto the side of the main house.

Stones protrude from the wall, and I can picture the old farmer and his wife hoisting themselves up to reach the eggs on a snowy winter morning. To think of those chickens, long before the USA was a country of her own, and now my own chickens makes me smile.

Hillside, long ago, had twelve structures listed on the property. By the time Bob and I got to it, only eleven of the buildings were still standing in some capacity. The grounds were so overgrown with trees and brush that we could not readily see what was on the land.

In our hunt to find the remains of the old buildings, we came across the stone ruins and the original old millstone. The stone was enormous! Bob had a crane move it from where we'd found it to the entrance of the barn for my birthday. Now it serves as a sort of "welcome mat" for everyone entering the new barn.

The Old Millstone

Clearing the land, a family affair...

We hired my younger brother and his friend to clear out brush and over 200 trees during their summer break. He often jokes that he never wants to see a wood chipper again. The painting jobs alone took a year. The rest of the property took yet *another* year.

Building on the ruins...

The new barn, which we built on the foundation of the old ruins, is a casual space to gather, watch movies on the projector, and host lively game nights. We've paired the rustic wood interior with warm rugs, soft leather cowhides, and plenty of wool blankets in the winter.

On the left-hand side of the barn doors, we have an ongoing list of every event we've hosted, from weddings, to Thanksgivings, to ping-pong tournaments.

MAKING A HOME

Definition of homemaking:

"the creation and management of a home, especially as a pleasant place in which to live."

Our houses serve us, not the other way around.

Bob and I took our time planning how the finished property should look. Hillside is a farm, not an estate. It's wild and free by nature, but we wanted that freedom to grow out of a solid structure. Even wild things can be orchestrated and have a clear flow. In our opinion, this is the greatest sort of beauty.

We wanted defined, intimate spaces in the vastness. All over the property, you'll find Adirondack chairs and benches nestled under trees and between beds of flowers. Outdoor dining and living spaces echo indoor ones with fire pits and fireplaces. Our goal was to make it easy for our family and guests to be together comfortably.

Beyond the living spaces, I wanted every single place your eye looked to house something thoughtful and lovely. Behind cabinet doors, in hidden nooks and crannies, nestled on stone walls, we've displayed the words that matter most and artwork that makes us happy.

Make your home yours. How you fill your home's spaces should be a celebration of people and comfort.

Aesthetics matter, but... what you like matters too. I love to choose something wonderful that catches my imagination, a rug, a special antique, a brilliant quilt, etc., and build my room around that piece.

Don't get stuck with one pattern or texture. A dramatic wallpaper, different textured surfaces on the floor and counters, cowhides, plaids, and florals all go together in my book. Even supposedly "different" styles (say, modern and colonial) can complement one another if tastefully selected.

VIRGINIA TECH
GOOD LIFE
THE RED TENT
CONVERSION
Born Again

"CHILDREN growing up in an atmosphere where beauty is considered an important part of daily life cannot help being inspired to develop their own original ideas in these areas, nor can they help being prepared to live aesthetically themselves. There is a 'togetherness' in sharing a prepared table that even very small children feel, although they cannot express it verbally." –Edith Schaeffer

I've chosen to frame the paintings and drawings my kids produce and hang them throughout the house. I want my children to understand that what they do matters, whether it is beautiful or not, and their creativity is worthy of respect and honor.

Choose complementary colors, mix old and new, choose the right color lightbulbs (not too bright or white!), bring in natural fibers, invest in pieces that inspire you, and... study designers you love and emulate their style. My personal favorites include Ralph Lauren, Charlotte Moss, Roman and Ivy, Richard Shapiro, and Pepper Tree Living. Their styles are classic, but they are not afraid to make bold decisions.

Even usually overlooked spaces like the linen closet or the landing to a staircase provide opportunities for joy. I've made the upstairs linen closet a space to display old family quilts and heirlooms alongside everyday sheets and towels. Meanwhile, every landing is a "frame" for my collection of hand-hooked rugs.

Finally, do things your way. You don't have to do things like everyone else. We don't have a guest book. Rather, we have our guests carve their names into the "guest log" in the barn. We also make memories out of doorposts and turn bathroom walls into scrapbooks.

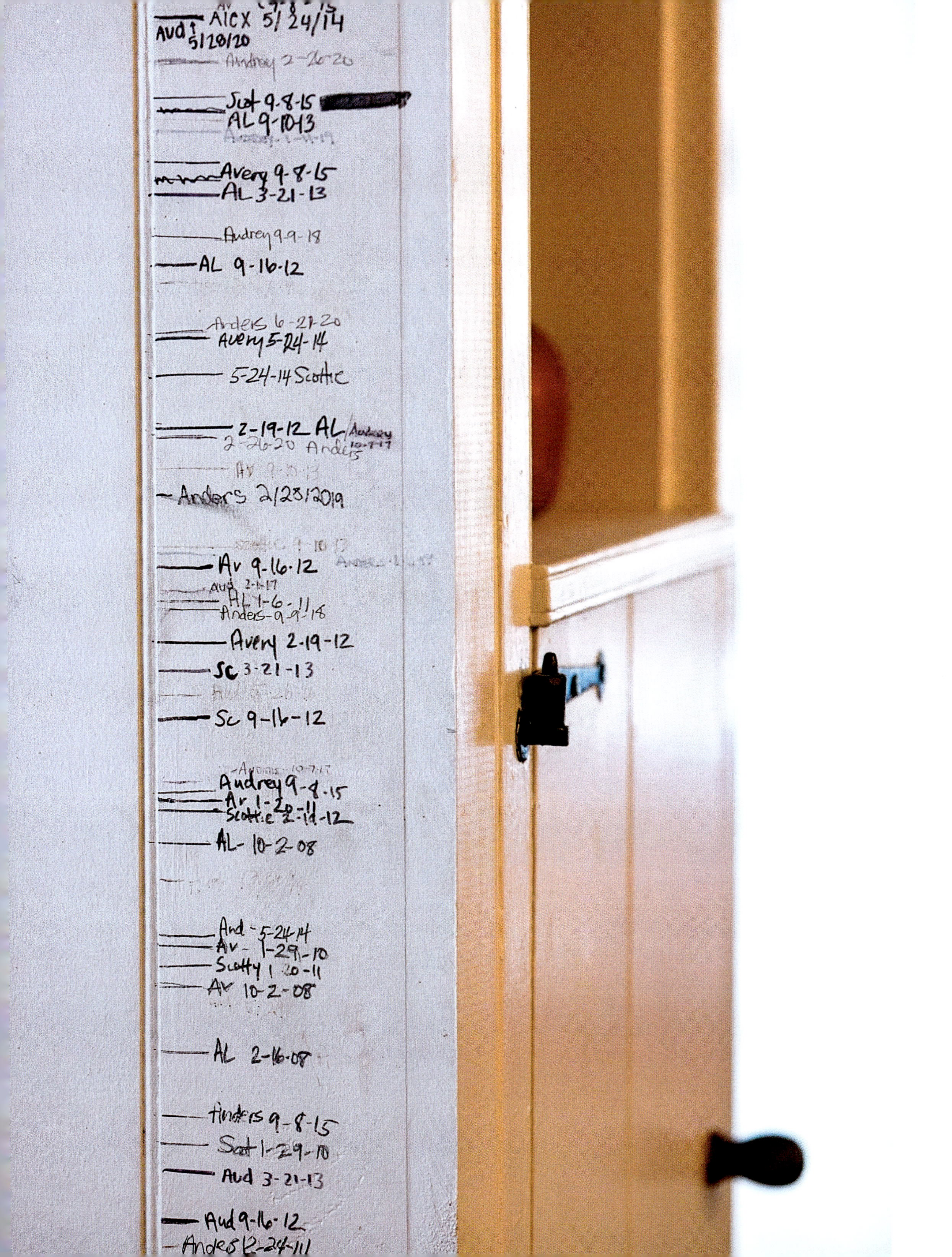
Alex 5/24/14
Aud 5/28/20
Audrey 2-26-20
Scot 9-8-15 [redacted]
AL 9-10-13
Avery 9-8-15
AL 3-21-13
Audrey 9-9-18
AL 9-16-12
Anders 6-27-20
Avery 5-24-14
5-24-14 Scottie
2-19-12 AL
2-26-20 Anders
Anders 2/28/2019
Av 9-16-12
AL 1-6-11
Anders 9-9-18
Avery 2-19-12
Sc 3-21-13
Sc 9-16-12
Audrey 9-8-15
Scottie 2-19-12
AL 10-2-08
Aud 5-24-14
Av 1-29-10
Av 10-2-08
AL 2-16-08
Anders 9-8-15
Scot 1-29-10
Aud 3-21-13
Aud 9-16-12

A Sense of Home

While the heart of "feeling at home" comes from the people who live in the house, there are things you can do to help the process along. Don't downplay the importance of our senses. Atmosphere and surroundings matter. And the more you can "sense" hominess with your five senses (smell, taste, touch, sight, and sound), the more at home you, your guests, and your family will be.

The Sweet Smell of Home

The smell of home changes from season to season. In summer, fresh herbs. In spring, flowers. In autumn and winter, the smell of the fireplace and mulling spices. And of course, the smell of something sweet baking is a welcome scent any time of year.

The Taste of Home

At our house, the taste of home is more about being together than a specific taste. But, truth be told, there is nothing quite like a home-cooked meal to make you feel at home. Fresh-baked cookies are, to me, the true taste of home.

Above, Picnic Berry Pie (P. 224)
Chocolate Chip Cookies (P. 105)

The Feel of Home

Texture is an important, and often overlooked, element in helping people feel at home. Soft couches, thick rugs on the floor, warm blankets... Every surface matters.

There really aren't any rules if the final product makes you happy. Mixing and matching patterns create a sense of relaxed beauty.

Top: This painting of Hillside Farm was painted in the early 1900s and was given to us by the grand-nieces and nephews of the owner and architect, Brognard Okie.

Middle: I had this painting of Hillside done for Bob as a "thank you" when he finished working on the house.

It's all in the details...

The Look of Home

Every space in your home provides a window into your personality. I try to make everywhere you can see a "feast for the eyes." This is all about setting and creativity. The unexpected promotes joy. Paint a bench red for a pop of color. Antiques mixed with modern pieces surprise and delight. My favorite part of my old-fashioned kitchen is the enormous modern painting over the kitchen table. Think retro and modern, big and small. And don't forget the lighting. Warm light from fireplaces, candles, and lamps adds atmosphere to every room.

Right: This painting is of me and Bob enjoying an afternoon on the Thames. I had it painted as a "thank you" gift when we flipped our first house. Turning memories into art is one of my favorite ways to commemorate precious moments.

S. LAWSON

The Sound of Home

Home is not complete without the sound of kids laughing, friends talking and having fun, and music. Music, music, music! Whether it's a quiet family meal or a large party, music is a must.

The Restful Home

HOME is meant to be a place of rest and renewal, even more so when it comes to the rooms where we sleep. Cool colors, soft, all-natural linens, heavy down-comforters, removing electronics, and lavender or eucalyptus-scented candles all contribute to a peaceful space. That said, no matter how peaceful and serene we've made our living spaces, true rest is found in our daily rhythms and our thought-life. We need to take time to feed our spirits and souls in order to reduce anxiety-producing thoughts. We need a full day off every week so we aren't running on empty when Monday rolls around. We need time to connect with our Creator and close friends and family on a heart level, daily if possible, so we don't bear our burdens alone.

The Master Bedroom

The Boys Room

WOLF

Given its architectural significance and brilliant design, Hillside stands on its own as a piece of art and American history. But the farm was never intended to be a museum piece. Its purpose has always been to provide a safe space to experience warmth, nourishment, and hope.

To say our kitchen is the heart of our home may sound cliché, but it is the truth. It's where the day begins and where it ends. It's a safe haven for important conversations and a welcome platform for the raucous laughter that comes from friends who truly know and love each other well.

There is something uniquely wonderful about the warmth of a kitchen and the safety and acceptance it provides. It's where real life happens, where the kids do homework and work out squabbles, where we eat breakfast and cook dinner.

My counter always has jars filled with candy and nuts. For younger guests, this is one of the favorite reasons they want to visit.

True hospitality is a sacred art. It has the power to heal and restore, to comfort and soothe. A sensitive homemaker makes her floor sacred ground because she has taken the time to make sure her family and guests feel understood, welcomed, and wanted when they are standing on it.

In every home that we have flipped, one of my non-negotiables is that we put a fireplace in the kitchen. In one house, there were no free walls, so we designed a pizza oven/fireplace for the countertop with a brick chimney reaching to the ceiling.

THE basic comforts of home, from the bedspread to the candles to the cookies, are all gifts from God. When we recognize our homes as places of opportunity to bless others, we begin a beautiful journey towards true family and community. This journey begins, however, only when we stop and take the time to share the gifts He's given us.

As a mother and a host, my goal is to make my home a safe place so my family and my guests have the opportunity to have deeper needs met. Intentional homemaking, in its most idealized form, is creating a setting where vulnerability and honesty are valued and protected, where understanding and grace are fostered, and love freely given.

Sharing Your Home Is a Blessing

Our heart has always been to have an open home. There have been years when we have had guests every other day. No matter how big or how small, no matter how little or much you have to share, an open home blesses not only those you welcome inside but your family as well.

Conversation, food, generosity, and presence are the soul of the home. Our world is a crazy one. While a meal cannot meet the needs of loneliness, feeling heard, or healing hearts, it can contribute to helping people truly connect. This is why the role of a host and homemaker is so important.

At Home in the Great Outdoors

I love making our outdoor spaces as comfortable and inviting as the indoor spaces.

I throw plaid blankets catty-corner over outdoor tables and line the benches with sheepskins for warmth and a little extra cushion. Candles, flowers, and good lighting are the final touches to feeling completely at home while outside.

Hillside is where we found home, not because of the house itself but because of the life and beauty we experience within its walls.

Over the years, the farm has been the site of family reunions, weddings, endless laughter, and a few tears. Everyone fits inside Hillside. Everyone is welcome. Every corner holds a memory. Every object, meaning.

Hillside is where Bob and I snuggle in front of the fire and dream up our next project. It's where the kitchen door is always open, rain or shine, night or day. It's where there is time for mulled cider and warm chocolate chip cookies and long talks with neighbors and family. It's where our children want to be with their friends.

The Guest

YOU MAY assume I grew up cooking with my mother like so many who write cookbooks. That was not my story. My mom dreaded cooking and any kind of formal entertaining. In fact, our family jokes that if she'd ever written a cookbook, it would have been called, "Dried or Blackened." What my mom did give me was a love for people, and that is more important than making a perfect dish.

Having everything "perfect" or "complete" is irrelevant. In fact, striving after perfection can wind up sucking all the joy from a celebration. The more you let go of perfection, the more you welcome real joy into hosting, whether it's for one or 100.

That said, while I don't strive for perfection, I do strive to bless my guests and make them feel as welcome and valued as possible.

In winter, I want people to feel physically warm… so we provide plenty of wool, fleece, and tartan blankets to cuddle up in around the fire. In the barn, we have sheepskin rugs on the benches to cut the chill. In the summer, we provide plenty of cold drinks.

Create a beautiful, quiet place for your guest to sleep. Crisp clean sheets, fluffy pillows, stacks of magazines and books, a candle, and a fresh bouquet of flowers say, "I want you here," whether your guest is staying in a private guest room or on your couch. It's helpful to spend a night where your guest will sleep before they arrive to make sure it is comfortable.

I like to find out my guest's favorite candy and leave it on their pillow. I've even had toiletry kits monogrammed with my guest's initials! Of course, what you do does not have to be extravagant. It simply needs to make your guest feel as though you've thought of them in advance. Something as easy to do as baking a tray of chocolate chip cookies.

HAVING A GUEST is worth celebrating because people are worth celebrating. A little extra preparation goes a long way. Do more than what is deemed "necessary." I want everyone who stays in my home to feel abundant blessing, from the bathroom to the kitchen table.

As a host, my goal in any event is to provide a space for fun, laughter, and memories… In other words, I want to provide a space for life, which, while sometimes imperfect, is always beautiful.

GUEST-READY
RECIPES

Ruth's Barely-Baked Chocolate Chip Cookies!

The lovely thing about cookie dough is everyone wants to lick the bowl. It's sweet. Salty. Decadent. I went on a quest to find a cookie twenty years ago that maintains that doughy goodness of cookie dough, and thanks to Lisa, this is the result. The key is to take them out of the oven the second the edges turn brown. It's won every informal competition among friends, and they call these "Ruth's Barely-Baked."

4 sticks butter
2 tablespoons vanilla
3 eggs
1 cup sugar
2½ cups brown sugar
1½ teaspoons salt
1½ teaspoons baking soda
5 cups flour
1 bag of good chocolate chips (I use Ghirardelli)

Step 1: Soften the butter until partially melted. Stir in brown sugar, sugar, vanilla, and eggs.
Step 2: Combine salt, baking soda, and flour in a bowl.
Step 3: Add the wet ingredients to the dry ingredients and mix by hand. Do not over mix! Stir in chocolate chips.
Step 4: Using an ice cream scoop, spoon generous balls of cookie dough onto a greased and lined baking sheet. Refrigerate at least 30 minutes (or overnight).
Step 5: When you are ready to bake, preheat the oven to 375°F on the convection setting.
Step 6: Put the cold cookie dough tray into the oven and bake until the edges are brown but centers are still gooey (about 10 minutes). They will look "barely-baked."

RUTH'S PRO-TIP
I often double or triple this recipe and freeze the raw dough in pre-scooped balls so we can have warm cookies whenever the mood strikes.

a piece of cake is the
ultimate welcome

Vanilla Bundt Cake with Chocolate Chips, P. 108

"Welcome" Chocolate Bundt Cake

I have my lovely sister-in-law to thank for this recipe that is chocolatey beyond description. This is, unsurprisingly, Bob's favorite birthday cake and one I often bake to welcome visitors. It is very rich.

The base is chocolate cake mix that gets kicked up a notch with the addition of sour cream and a box of chocolate pudding mix. And because we take our chocolate very seriously around here, I throw in a handful of the best chocolate chips I can find just for kicks.

When that first bite of chocolate perfection hits your tongue, you'll thank me.

1 box chocolate cake mix (I use devil's food)
1 cup oil
4 eggs
1 cup sour cream
1 cup water
1 large box instant chocolate pudding
6 oz. chocolate chips

Step 1: Preheat the oven to 325°F.
Step 2: Thoroughly grease a bundt pan.
Step 3: Combine all the ingredients together until smooth and pour into the prepared pan.
Step 4: Bake for 45-50 minutes or until a toothpick comes out clean.

Vanilla Bundt Cake with Chocolate Chips

1 box vanilla cake mix
1 cup oil
4 eggs
1 cup sour cream
1 cup water
1 large box instant vanilla pudding
8 oz. chocolate chips

Step 1: Preheat the oven to 325°F.
Step 2: Thoroughly grease a bundt pan.
Step 3: Combine all the ingredients together until smooth and pour into the prepared pan.
Step 4: Bake for 45-50 minutes or until a toothpick comes out clean.

Goldrush Coffee Cake

I make this coffee cake for every holiday and shower. It is adapted from Panera's Cinnamon Crumb Coffee Cake recipe by Maris Callahan and is so good that my kids have asked for it in lieu of a birthday cake!

So... what makes it such a standout?

First off, it's gorgeous. The streusel runs right through the middle. When you take a bite, you'll think you've struck a vein of sweet, buttery, golden goodness.

Secondly, it might be the most moist coffee cake I've ever had.

This cake is not difficult on the baking scale and uses everyday ingredients you probably already have on hand. What's more, it lasts on the counter for a few days (well... not in my house) and serves as a beautiful gift if you want to make something special for someone you love.

Serve with strong coffee. And if you're feeling extra decadent, dollop with thick homemade whipped cream.

MIX YOUR STREUSEL

½ cup granulated sugar
⅔ cup lt. brown sugar, lightly packed
2 teaspoons ground cinnamon
¼ teaspoon ground nutmeg
2 sticks unsalted butter, melted
2⅔ cups all-purpose flour

Combine the granulated sugar, brown sugar, cinnamon, and nutmeg in a bowl. Stir in the melted butter and then the flour. Mix well and set aside.

(continued on the next page...)

PREPARE YOUR BATTER

12 (1½ sticks) tablespoons unsalted butter, room temperature
1½ cups granulated sugar
4 large eggs, room temperature
2 teaspoons pure vanilla extract
1⅓ cups sour cream
2½ cups all-purpose flour
2 teaspoons baking powder
½ teaspoon baking soda
1 teaspoon kosher salt

Step 1: Preheat the oven to 350°F. Butter and flour a 9-inch round bundt pan.
Step 2: Cream the butter and sugar in the bowl of an electric mixer on high-speed for 4 to 5 minutes, until light.
Step 3: Reduce the speed to low and add the eggs, one at a time. Then slowly add the vanilla and sour cream.
Step 4: In a separate bowl, sift together the flour, baking powder, baking soda, and salt.
Step 5: Slowly add the flour mixture to the batter until just combined.
Step 6: Mix with a spatula to be sure the batter is completely mixed.
Step 7: Spoon half of the batter into the prepared bundt pan and spread it out with a knife.
Step 8: With your fingers, crumble half of the topping evenly over the batter.
Step 9: Pour in the remainder of the batter and crumble the remaining half of the streusel topping on top. Bake for 40 to 50 minutes until a cake tester comes out clean. Cool completely before serving.

Goldrush Coffee Cake, Rustic Summer Blueberry Tart (P. 227)

Give of Oneself

Remember, being a good host is a matter of the heart, not a checkbook. "Silver and gold have I none, but such as I have, giveth thee," is one of my favorite verses in Scripture. What I have to give that truly matters comes from who I am, not what I have.

How can you give of who you are to those in your home, be they a family member or a guest?

Be Together
Stay Present
Stay Generous
Show Compassion
Welcome new friendships
Have an "Open House" to children and grownups alike.
Experience Rest
Feed the Soul (Bake Often!)
Serve Abundantly
Value others and what they value
Have fun and play often
Cheer one another on, especially in the tough times.
Laugh Easily
Let go of Perfection

The more people you have in your home, the dirtier it will get. I will always choose a full house over a clean one. Don't be afraid of the messes people bring. And don't be alarmed if you find yourself always cleaning up one mess or another. This is a clear sign that your home is full of life, and a healthy home is a lively one. Final thoughts? Don't be afraid to let others see the mess. It doesn't mean you haven't prepared. It just means that you are transparent. Letting people in on your mess creates closeness and lets people know you are comfortable going to places that aren't perfect. It lets people know you are open to real-life friendships.

Something to celebrate...

EVERY good party starts with something to celebrate. There are the basics—holiday parties, birthday parties, and victory celebrations. And then there are those parties we throw just for the sake of gathering together and having a wonderful time. I am a firm believer that the privilege of sharing life with our friends and family is reason enough to throw open the doors to my kitchen, welcome the neighborhood, and turn the music up.

The premiere of a favorite show, a football game, or a movie night are all perfect opportunities to set up the projector in the barn and invite a bunch of friends over for an informal night in our makeshift theater. These evenings are not complete without buttered popcorn and plenty of hot chocolate to go around.

More formal reasons to celebrate, like graduations and anniversaries, are worth putting forth a little more effort than usual. We set the table with the good china and get a little more dressed up than our everyday. I think making things special and setting aside times to celebrate one another is one of the sweetest and most memorable parts of being a part of a family.

Every so often, I give the "hostess reins" to my kids. They love throwing parties for their friends and choosing the decor, menu, and activities for the event. From waffle parties with all the fixings followed by a scary movie to Ice Cream Sundae Sundays and pie-making sessions followed by a mini etiquette class, the barn has become the fun hub in the neighborhood.

I want my kids and their friends to feel completely comfortable and welcome at my house. I'd rather that they spend their time at Hillside than anywhere else. As my Aunt Andrea taught me, and experience has proved time and time again, you never have to have the biggest or best house if you want teenagers hanging out, you just have to have the best food and plenty of it.

PLANNING AHEAD

NOTHING can ruin a party more than a frazzled host. The key to avoiding this problem is to plan ahead. There are several women in my life who have taught me the fine art of party-preparation (Gillian, Llonka, and Aunt Kim, I'm looking at you!). Believe me, if you follow these tips, you will actually have fun at your own party and get to focus on what really matters... your guests!

There are always times for spur-of-the-moment parties. For those, I pick up the phone or shoot a group text the morning of. It's usually best, however, to give your guests time to make space in their schedules so they can plan ahead to come. We always send out email reminders to keep people up-to-date on times and locations.

Choose your serving dishes two or three days before your party. Invest in a few large boards for cheese and charcuterie platters and big bowls for salads and pastas. I love to go to flea markets and find unique (and food safe) porcelain, pewter, and wood dishes.

SET your tables the day before the event. This includes your buffet tables and your flower arrangements. I keep a cabinet full of candles, vases, and other decorative table items ready to go so I have a range of options to choose from, even for last-minute gatherings. It's always smart to have a bunch of tea candles on hand. They make any table look elegant in seconds.

The backyard is a secret treasure trove for floral arrangements. You will be shocked by what you can find to give your arrangements a raw, natural beauty!

When it comes to flowers, your arrangements depend on your party-setting and the level of formality you are aiming for. Rooms with tall ceilings demand tall arrangements. We like to incorporate branches and foliage from the property to fill out the space. In spring and summer, it's lovely to use wildflowers. I have peonies and magnolias that are magnificent for months. They give floral arrangements a wonderful whimsical touch that runs parallel to the season. In autumn, I always bring in pumpkins and gourds. In winter, I use branches from fir trees and holly berries. These classic touches make everyone feel at home.

It's all in the presentation...

I've never understood why people had stacks of china in their cabinets but never used them. While I love the ease of cleanup that comes with paper plates, I also love to make "everyday" dinners a special occasion by pulling out the cloth napkins, placemats, chargers, and fancy wine glasses. Our time on earth is short, so why not go the extra mile every once in a while?

I tend to only buy white tablecloths, napkins, and dishes because they go with any setting, color palette, or season. It doesn't matter if they come from the same collection or not, white dishes always go together. I consider my dishes and linens a blank canvas that I can dress up with different floral arrangements, fun chargers, placemats, and lots of candles.

Collecting Impressions

There is a challenge and reward connected to collecting, as well as a secret pleasure in presenting a table filled with unique pieces that whimsically work together. I love collections. Baskets. Breadboards. Salt and pepper shakers. Cream and sugar holders. Silver napkin rings.

These collections have grown over the years through flea market finds and gifts from family and friends who know me well, and they make appearances at almost every gathering. The boards are perfect for presenting cheeses and charcuterie, desserts, and cream and sugar for coffee. My baskets, tipped to the side, become cornucopias for assorted breads, crackers, and chips. Tray baskets are ideal for displaying napkins and cutlery for larger buffets. Remember: you don't have to use an item the way it was intended. It's all in the presentation.

Collecting for Hosting:

- Bread Boards
- Pottery Mugs
- Wooden Bowls
- Baskets
- Vases (of all shapes and sizes)
- Depression Glass
- Crystal Cut Wine Glasses
- Candle Holders or Silver Candlesticks
- Mixed Antique Cutlery (silver-plated is cheap and beautiful!)
- Porcelain Teacups and Dessert Plates
- Milk Bottles

Don't forget that you can literally build your own collection from scratch. Several years ago, Bob cut down a tree on the property that's trunk was the perfect circumference to serve as chargers. Bob sliced the trunk into 20 rounds and burned "Hillside Farm" into each one. In the same vein, I once received a leather hide as a birthday present, which Bob cut into squares for placemats. When building a collection, there is lots of room for innovation and creativity.

HOW do you build a unique collection of your own? Start with local flea markets, antique stores, garage sales, and estate sales.

On Saturdays, Bob and I used to load up the strollers with the kids, grab a coffee, and hit the garage sales in all the great neighborhoods in our area. It was a weekly date! He would pretend to enjoy sifting through junk looking for treasures, just for me. (These excursions yielded a special collection of china teacups for each child. Each time we have "tea" at our house, everyone gets to use their favorite cup.)

Many of the sellers on Etsy and other similar sites have done the hard work of finding beautiful dishes and flatware for you. You don't have to spend much to start a fantastic collection! Then, the next time you throw a party, pull out your special finds. Not only will they beautify your setting, but they will serve as wonderful conversation pieces.

I LOVE sharing my collections with my kids as a way to pass down a little piece of myself. Every year, I give my daughters one antique silver napkin ring from my collection. By the time they are grown and out of the house, they'll each have their own unique collection that reminds them of their childhood.

HILLSIDE
BLESS

WHEN throwing a formal party for any number over 12, I rent dishes. You may hesitate just like I did, thinking it will be expensive, but call your local party rental, and I promise, they will have something to fit your budget. The big plus is you don't even have to wash the dishes. You put them back in the bins, and they take them away to wash them. Believe me, renting china is much easier than spending all night washing up. I also pull on my kids and my friends to help with set-up and tear-down. There is no reason to exhaust yourself by doing everything on your own. And truth be told, people love getting to help. Some of my sweetest friendships have been forged in party-preparation and party-clean-up mode.

How to build a cheese board...

Start with a variety of soft cheese, hard cheese, and blue cheese. I like a goat or triple cream Brie for my soft cheese, a Gruyere for my hard cheese, and a Gorgonzola or Stilton for my blue cheese. Pair with:

FRUIT
Add fresh grapes, sliced apples and pears, dried apricots, strawberries, figs, a pomegranate, etc.

NUTS
Marcona almonds, spiced cashews, chocolate-covered almonds, salted pecans, fresh walnuts, candied nuts, pistachios, etc.

CURED MEATS
Salami, chorizo, prosciutto, etc.

BREAD AND CRACKERS
Sliced baguettes and rustic country loaves, rice crackers, flatbread crisps, water crackers, etc.

SWEETS AND SAVORIES
Honey, fig jam, onion jam, olive oil, and balsamic vinegar, plus olives, spicy pickles, etc.

A well-stocked pantry and fridge makes the CHEESE BOARD an instant light meal or appetizer for surprise guests. I like to keep a few cheeses, crackers, and nuts on hand, just in case someone unexpected arrives at the farm.

Party-Ready Appetizers

Lori's Decadent Party Cheese Dip

My cousin Lori shared the best dip recipe for festive gatherings. The creamy flavor is complemented by salty, crispy bacon goodness. It's a beautiful addition to any cheese board and adds an element of fun to otherwise predictable appetizer spreads.

1 bar of cracker barrel reserve New York cheddar (or any other kind you have on hand)
1 small package sliced almonds
1 bunch of green onions
1 cup Hellmann's mayo
1 jar Hormel real bacon bits

Step 1: Grate the cheese.
Step 2: Chop the onions and mix all ingredients until well combined.
Step 3: Shape into a ball and serve alongside your favorite crackers.

RUTH'S PRO-TIP
Instead of forming the mixture into a ball, I sometimes like to spoon it into a mason jar alongside my favorite cheeses on a charcuterie board.

Double-Cheese Stuffed Mushrooms

These make an unbelievably great appetizer for any dinner party, especially in the cooler months. They have the perfect amount of richness (and are so easy to make) that I find myself serving them at nearly every holiday gathering. Trust me, even non-mushroom lovers will be tempted!

1 lb. white button mushrooms (you could also use Baby Bells)
8 oz. cream cheese
1 cup grated parmesan
1 teaspoon Worcestershire
1 teaspoon dried dill

Step 1: Preheat oven to 350°F.
Step 2: Clean the mushrooms and remove the stems.
Step 3: Mix the rest of the ingredients together.
Step 4: Spoon the mixture into each individual mushroom and place on a lined baking sheet.
Step 5: Bake for 20 minutes.

Serve warm.

TRADITIONS

Definition of tradition:

"an inherited, established, or customary pattern of thought, action, or behavior."

WHILE "out with the old, in with the new" certainly has its place, not everything is meant to be innovative. The tried and true is tried and true for a reason. Certain things just work. All you need to do is ask whether the tradition passes down faith, hope, and love. If the answer is "yes," it is a tradition worth keeping.

Beautiful traditions are some of the keys that separate houses from homes. Traditions have the power to hold families together in times of uncertainty, providing a sense of stability and regularity. They are both a heritage and a legacy no one can take from you or your children. Here are a few of ours.

We have special traditions for every holiday and season, but the following are unique traditions we follow any time of year. It's important to have regular traditions that make you smile and bring your family together.

FOR NEARLY 20 years, we have set aside time and space to read our favorite books together as a family several nights a week, continuing a tradition started by my parents. (Some of our family favorites include: *The Chronicles of Narnia*, *The Lord of the Rings*, *Boys in the Boat*, and *Unbroken*.) Of all our family traditions, this may be the collective favorite. What's more, this tradition has opened up the world of literature to our children and regularly brings us together to share not only in the experience of reading, but gives us a chance to decompress as a family and reflect on the day.

*To encourage the younger members of the family to sit quietly, we always have a few puzzles on hand for the listeners. We get cozy in front of a fire, whether inside of the house, outside by the fire pit, or around a campfire. We pour a mug or two of mulled cider or hot chocolate and dive into another world.

THE GOAL JAR

Twice a year, all the McKeaneys gather around the table to share their goals for the next six months. Each one writes down their goal, dates it, and puts it in our special "goal jar." For the kids, these goals range from academics, to sports, to spiritual growth. For Bob and I, they usually have something to do with a new project.

There is no reward for the goals we achieve, other than the internal reward of a job well done and a sense of personal accomplishment. Bob and I encourage a forward-thinking culture, desiring more than the status quo, and pushing past personal limits. And when we don't happen to succeed in meeting our set goals, we pick ourselves up, dust ourselves off, and try again.

"Next to trying and winning, the best thing is trying and failing."
– Lucy Maud Montgomery

THE SNOOTY GOODLE DANCE

At the beginning of our marriage, we put a lot of time into deciding what traditions we wanted to incorporate into the fabric of our family life. There were certain customs we grew up with that we wanted to pass down to our children. There were other areas where we went "untraditional" in order to create special traditions of our own. The Snooty Goodle (also known as the Tooth Fairy) happens to be one of the traditions passed down from my parents and grandparents.

The tradition essentially is this: when anyone loses a tooth, they are required to do a dance to a song of their choice (siblings are always welcome to join!). If they dance for an entire song, and if the Snooty Goodle deems it a worthy dance, he may leave some money underneath the pillow of the toothless child.

If my fireplace pleases thee,
As indeed it pleases me,
Sit a while and share its glow,
Peace take with thee when thou dost go.

HONORING THE PAST

ANDREW MITCHELL, my great grandfather, was a successful commercial artist in Southern California at the turn of the twentieth century. You might have seen his work on the famous Del Monte shield. In his time, he was considered one of America's most artistic penmen and turned many sayings into decorative wall plaques that are still sold today. A.E. Mitchell, as he was known, was passionate that our walls serve as a constant reminder of who we are, encouraging us to trust more, love better, and serve always. Our walls are filled with his reminders, designed in the 1920s and 1930s, linking us to our heritage and propelling us into our future. Bless; Together; Earth has No Sorrow that Heaven Cannot Heal; Others; Me Worry?; Never Give Up; and As for Me and My House, We will Serve the Lord have prominent places throughout my house and property.

Growing up, my favorite plaque of his was the "fireplace" plaque which hung in my grandfather's home. Though I don't know what happened to that particular plaque… it maintained its special space on the walls of my memory.

Several years ago, Bob and I were on vacation in Jackson Hole. On a whim, we pulled off the road at a flea market. Lo and behold, what did Bob find? A copy of my grandfather's "fireplace" plaque. It now hangs over our outdoor fireplace mantle in our stone ruins.

BIRTHDAY BALLOONS

EVERY birthday, we write special letters to bless the birthday child and "wrap" the door of their bedroom. It's a simple gesture, but one that showers the recipient with love and helps establish their important role as a member of the family. While they sleep, we fill their room with 100 balloons in whatever color happens to be the child's favorite that particular year. (There was that year that we had to dig up 100 cheetah print balloons because "cheetah" was the favorite color.)

We have five children between 11 and 20. That's five birthdays per year, 100 manually blown-up balloons per birthday. You do the math. We've blown up a lot of balloons. And we've continued this tradition even as the older children have gone to college. I don't know how he does it, but Bob has managed to fill more than one dorm room with 100 balloons. There is something magical about waking up every birthday to 100 balloons filling every square inch of a bedroom floor.

Birthdays are not something to be taken lightly, and some birthdays are even more special than others. When someone turns the big 16, we always give 16 gifts (ranging from a box of their favorite sugary cereal to their first cell phone) every hour through the day starting at 6 in the morning and ending at 10 at night, one gift an hour. (Their siblings have been known to interrupt classes at school to make birthday deliveries!)

Bob and I want our children to feel celebrated from the moment they wake up until the minute they fall asleep. We also knew we didn't want birthdays to be centered on big parties with dozens of friends. Rather, we opted to use birthdays as special times set aside for the family.

Seize any chance you have to re-focus on what really matters... how much you love one another, how much someone means to you. These moments create something to hold onto when more difficult times come (and they will) and memories that will last.

Happy Birthday alex
HAPPY 20th Birthday alex
ALEX
ALEX
YOU ARE 20.
WE LOVE YOU
It is your Birthday.
YOU ARE:
Goodbye teen

Leave room for fun and games

We've left space for play. Much of Hillside is still wooded, but we've cut a trail through the densest portions for go-karts and scavenger hunts. The lawn is cleared for flag football and relay races. And the zipline is always in season.

- Spike Ball
- Zipline
- Cornhole
- Basketball
- Football
- Flag Football
- 4-Square
- Tetherball
- Ping-Pong
- Trampolines
- Croquet
- Pickleball
- Bocce Ball
- Shuffle Ball
- Volleyball
- Foosball

There is a difference between legacy and heritage.

We all have a heritage. It's something we are born with and cannot change. But our legacy? That's up to us. We all have choices to make that will dictate what we leave behind when we pass.

Bob making cutting boards as a gift for one of our family reunions.

“EVERY FAMILY NEEDS TO BE REDISCOVERED”

"We need pioneers who ask hard questions about priorities and want to be more like a mountain stream that carves rock than a meandering muddy river close to the sea... clear direction, fiercely pursued with persistence, overcoming obstacles, climbing rocks, reaching the summit."

—Hubert Morken (Ruth's uncle)

Loving, supportive, generous homes don't just “happen.” Rather, they are the result of intentionality from all members. Take time to name what you value together. Your shared values will become your shared mission, and they will guide all of you through the ups and downs of life's journey.

Moments spent defining what matters to you as a family sets an incredible example to kids. It's never too early to start thinking about how to love one another better, serve others tirelessly, and stay true to what matters most.

To get the process started, ask one another what you value most. Then try to understand what makes your family come alive. Finally, summarize everyone's thoughts in a few sentences. Three to four is plenty.

We value hard work, fun, people, and adventure. Our mission is to love others well, welcome strangers into our home, and to live lives worthy of our Creator and serve Him all our days.

After developing your family values (it may need to go through a few revisions!), write them down and put them in a visible place in your house. As time goes by and you realize something in your family's daily rhythm is not lining up with your mission statement, you can gently adjust until everything is back in line.

a *year* at hillside

RECIPES, CELEBRATIONS,
AND SEASONAL TIPS

Spring

PLANTING SEASON

SPRING: the season that bursts with a promise of new life, warmth, and color after months of cold, ice, and grey. When the first sunny day strikes Hillside, birds break into song, new growth and pops of color jump out in every corner, and the lovely scent of fresh blossoms floats across the farm. It's marvelous.

It is also very busy. Preparing beds, choosing seedlings, planting, weeding... For several weeks, it is a constant hands-on project. Each plant needs gentle care, space, and just the right amount of sun and water. They sometimes remind me of children. Too much attention and they don't grow. Too little attention and they run wild. You have to strike the right balance, pray for help, and trust God to do the rest.

Without fail, the seeds we've planted shower us with joy as March turns to April and April to May. They continue through the heat of summer and well into autumn. And even when the rest of my garden begins to fade, my dahlias remain as cheery and colorful as the first day they bloomed, reminding me that no matter what the coming winter holds, spring lies just beyond it.

I wish I could say I've always loved gardening.

Truth be told, my relationship with green and growing things has been rocky and dry. For years, I associated yard work with getting into trouble. One way my parents disciplined was sending us out to weed the lawn. My distaste continued well into my marriage. We took pride in finding houses with no yards to take care of.

Needless to say, when we bought Hillside, with its acres and acres of untouched tangled woods and branches growing through the third story, I felt intimidated. Sure, we could redo a house in our sleep but restore an entire property? That was truly daunting. My love of gardening began slowly. A pot filled with herbs in my kitchen to be specific. Obviously, I love cooking. You could almost say my newfound joy in the garden came from my love of fresh herbs in tomato sauces and salads.

From there, Bob built me *The Herb Garden*, just a step down from the back door of the house.

The Herb Garden

The 15x15-foot plot with raised beds was modeled after a classic English garden. One year, I tried tomatoes, but I didn't like how messy they looked. Now, I stick with herbs mixed with flowers.

Function and Beauty

While I certainly enjoy gardening more than I used to, I still don't want to spend more time in the dirt than I need to. So I choose plants that grow easily and do not have to be replanted every year (goodbye annuals, hello perennials!). This also saves a lot of money in the long run.

Herbs, grown in your kitchen in a box or an herb garden, are always useful when dinnertime rolls around. I love to give pots filled with herbs as gifts for birthdays or showers. It's an edible arrangement that lasts for months.

First and foremost, when it comes to planting an unforgettably lovely garden, choose a color scheme. I suggest two complementary colors max—more than two—and you risk muddying the final visual effect. My colors are purple and white. You will see pops of purple all over the property through Catmint and lavender (where it will grow). The white comes through my hydrangea shrubs.

Your color scheme can extend even to functional garden spaces like herb gardens or orchards. Underneath each of my apple trees, we have a square bed of bright purple Catmint that comes up in spring and summer.

I've sporadically planted the herb garden with Allium. Alliums pop up randomly as bold pops of color between the basil and rosemary. I've also included a dark wine-colored Echinacea here and there, as well as dark purple tulips.

Looking past THE HERB GARDEN lies the rest of Hillside.

I knew the land (and there is a lot of it!) needed a plan, i.e., structure.

But I also didn't want the property to lose its natural wooded freedom. Hillside is a farm nestled in the woods at heart. We didn't want to force it into a predictable, manicured suburban mold.

Learning to garden is really about learning to trust. In February, everything looks dead. I had to learn to trust that the plants were just sleeping. There was a time in my checkered gardening past that I would see the hibernating branches and think they were dead because they looked dead. So... I would rip everything out and replant. Of course, they weren't dead. They were just resting. With the warmth of March, a hint of green always appears, followed by an explosion of color, providing evidence of life!

How often is this the case with our inner gardens?

When I say "inner gardens," I mean the garden of our hearts, the place where we dream, plan, and hope. We all have winter seasons, spring seasons, summer seasons, and harvest seasons. Each one is valuable and important. But some seasons, like winter, are harder than others.

It is difficult when we do not feel like we are bearing "fruit" and producing what we want, or our branches look dry and ugly, not covered with the glorious flowers of spring. But we must learn to embrace winter if we are to enjoy flowers and fruit. One does not come without the other, not in our inner gardens or outdoor gardens.

"A garden is a grand teacher.
It teaches patience and careful
watchfulness; it teaches
industry and thrift; above all it
teaches entire trust."

— Gertrude Jekyll

WHAT TO PLANT?

Some plants work better than others, depending on where you live and what kind of soil you have in your yard. My recommendation is to search online or go to your library and study up on what works best in your region. This will save you a lot of frustration in the long run.

I tried to plant Echinacea for three years in a row. It never grew the way it should in certain plots. Finally, we discovered our soil was too sandy, and only certain plants thrive in such sandy soil. In our case, we discovered that Catmint, onion grass, eucalyptus, and ferns love to grow at Hillside.

"Gardens are not made by singing, 'Oh how beautiful,' and sitting in the shade." —Rudyard Kipling

How to Plant a Window Box

- When building or purchasing a window box, make sure to measure your box so it is a few inches wider than the base of the window.
- Fill the box with good potting soil. (If it's an open wire box, line it with sheet moss before filling with soil.)
- When it comes to actually choosing my plants and flowers for a box, I go for a mixture of perennials and hearty annuals that can withstand the cold. A wonderful combination might be Creeping Jenny and salvia (both annuals) and some flowering perennials and short grass that hangs or drapes over the box. What plants you choose is dependent on light (sun versus shade). Don't expect plants or flowers that need hours in the sunlight to thrive if your box is on the shady side of the house. Succulents that flower and have different colored leaves are fun choices, but be aware that these require special soil and lots of sun. If your box sits in the shade most of the day, go for ferns, pansies, impatiens, Creeping Jenny, or variegated ivy. (In other words, do your research before you buy your plants!) *If you use perennials, at the end of the season replant them, and they can be used the following year.
- Don't forget to water your box every day (or run a drip irrigation system through it)! They will dry up quickly if forgotten.

WHEN planning a garden, choose your plants according to height and color. Choosing a "palette" of plants from high to low guides your eye and gives each plant space to shine visually. I incorporate lots of boxwoods and hydrangeas for structure and focus.

The high-to-low rule extends even to window boxes. Every season, we plant our window boxes according to the weather or holiday.

BY the time we got to Okie's front garden, it was primarily weeds and dead branches. We opted to strip everything out and start over. In the process, we found two rather remarkable discoveries.

The first was an inscription on the step leading down into the garden, "To raise flowers is a common thing. God alone gives them fragrance."

The second was a plaque in the stone retaining wall. It reads, "In Memory of Frank Monroe Thomas, Lover and Maker of Gardens, Who Died for His Country in France in 1918."

It seemed that no one had truly cared for the garden since that young gardener had passed away decades before.

It was once more time to love and make a garden. Where better than where a garden had been loved and made by a hero so long ago?

There was almost a spiritual significance to restoring the property and bringing it back to life. We gave ourselves grace to learn and make mistakes, settled in for the long haul, choosing not to try and finish everything at once, and opted to focus on one section of the property at a time. It took several years to get our bearings. For one thing, it takes time for plants to grow. It's a "sleep, creep, and leap" process. But in the end, our garden grew into a piece of heaven.

WERS IS A COMMON THING
E GIVES THEM FRAGRANCE

The Flowers in My Garden

ASIATIC AND CASABLANCA LILIES The Flowers of Purity
CORNFLOWERS The Flower of Friendship
VERONICAS The Flower of Fidelity
DAHLIAS The Flower of Enduring Grace
SALVIA The Flower of Thoughtfulness
THISTLES The Flower of Bravery
YARROWS The Flower of Inspiration
ROSES The Flower of Love
IRISES The Flower of Wisdom
PEONIES The Flower of Honor
SHASTA DAISIES The Flower of Innocence
BULBS OF ALLIUM The Flower of Prosperity
ASTILBES The Flower of Patience
TALL CARNATIONS The Flower of Gratitude

The Cutting Garden

Not long ago, Bob built me a special fenced-in garden specifically for cutting flowers—flowers used in arrangements. This garden is not held to the "two-color" rule that applies to the rest of the property. Deep reds, sunset oranges, and soft yellows clash with the electric pinks and purples of hearty annuals. It is a cacophony of color.

Why does one need a cutting garden, you might ask, if you have flowers and greenery adorning the rest of your yard or beds? The answer is simple: the purpose of a cutting garden is for harvesting. The purpose of flowers planted around your home is meant for just that, to add color and form to your yard. Those flowers are not meant to be clipped. Their blooms belong in the great outdoors. Not so with the cutting garden. These blooms are specifically meant to be cut and brought inside by the armload.

HOW TO PLANT A CUTTING GARDEN

Choose a sunny spot in your yard.

Build a raised bed (also called a container). You may need to fence in your garden if you have deer in your region.

Line the bottom of your container with stones.

Fill your container with a high-quality potting mix.

Plant your flowers!

- Spring is the best time to plant, but some flowers do fine in the autumn. Remember, in the spring, do not plant your flowers until the last frost date is over.

- Choose a day that is overcast and not too hot or bright. Rain is ideal!

- Plant your flowers in clumps for easy cutting.

Water your container daily at first, then every other day, and then every third day.

Enjoy beautiful fresh flowers for months at a time!

It is best to start growing perennials from nursery plants. They are difficult to start successfully from seed. Plant in early autumn, ideally several weeks before the first frost. If you choose to plant them in spring, they will grow, however, they will not be as productive their first year. In general, perennials take several years to reach maturity. As such, it's important to keep their beds weeded and well-tended to early on.

Dividing perennials from time to time gives their root systems room to grow and encourages them to bloom. These divisions can be used to start new flower beds or can be splendid gifts. There is something lovely about visiting a friend and knowing that the flowers in their garden are "sister-plants" of yours. In early fall or spring, carefully dig up one of your plants (it helps if the soil is well-moistened to loosen the roots) and shake off the soil from the roots. Carefully pull or cut the plant into two parts. Each part should have its own root system and leaves. Replant each section at roughly the same depth they were when you uprooted them.

EASTER *at Hillside...*

42 years ago,

MY mother started a tradition that is possibly one of the most important traditions of all that we do on Easter: the Easter Treasure Hunt.

It started as a simple treasure hunt in the backyard with clever clues and a handful of candy. But over the last four decades, it has grown into an epic adventure that takes several hours and ends with a grand cash prize and a treasure trove of sugar. Depending on where we spend the holiday, the clues have led through cities, around amusement parks, and even through museums.

These days, it's my father who's in charge. It takes him days to prepare. He chooses the place, the time, and organizes the teams. Every team is given the first riddle. Some sort of competition, such as shooting arrows or a three-legged race, determines which team gets a head start. From there, everyone descends upon the set location of the hunt.

Over the years, we've found the grand prize in the middle of a lake, in the ocean, and even up a chimney. No hiding place is too wild.

To celebrate, the winners share the candy, and we all settle in for a giant Mexican feast.

Hillside Farm has become such a sweet home for our family. It's also become home to many friendly chickens who pay us rent in the form of daily eggs.

I'm confident that somewhere in-between the hundreds of batches of scrambled eggs I've made, I've come pretty close to perfection. Seriously, we make eggs every day… If not for breakfast, we make them for dinner. The naughtiness of dinner! Who made the rule that eggs are just for breakfast?

The New Chicken Coup

Scrambled Eggs for Seven 

Though eggs in and of themselves are naturally rich and filling, we bring it up a notch or two by gently melting in a bit of cream cheese just as the eggs finish cooking. You won't believe how creamy and smooth they become. You'll never go back to scrambling any other way.

12 eggs
¼ cup half-and-half
⅓ package cream cheese (cut into bite-sized pieces)
salt and pepper

Step 1: Melt butter into a large skillet on medium-low.
Step 2: Crack eggs into a large bowl and whisk with half-and-half.
Step 3: Gently pour into the skillet and stir constantly with a silicone spatula.
Step 4: Just before the eggs set, stir in cream cheese.
Step 5: Salt and pepper to taste. Serve alone or on thick buttered toasted brioche.

Cheese Quiche

There's a French bakery nearby that makes a quiche that is thicker and cheesier and more delicious than any other quiche I've ever had. Luckily, they shared their secret with me: cover the bottom crust with a generous handful of cheese and then pour your custard on top.

Quiche is a great dish in general, but this recipe just might take the crown. Instead of being a typical flat (and tasteless) quiche, this one is four inches high and filled with melted, sharp cheddar. At our house, it makes for a light lunch or a quick dinner (and helps put all those eggs our chickens produce to good use).

8 eggs, lightly beaten
3 cups sour cream or heavy cream (or equal parts of both)
1½ cups sharp cheddar cheese
a pinch of ground nutmeg
1 teaspoon salt
½ teaspoon pepper

"A Very English Crust," rolled a quarter-inch thick and pressed into a 9-inch pie pan (P. 272).

Step 1: Preheat the oven to 375°F.
Step 2: Mix together the eggs, cream, nutmeg, and salt and pepper.
Step 3: Shred the cheese and layer the bottom of the crust.
Step 4: Pour the egg mixture over the cheese.
Step 5: Bake for 45 minutes and then cover with tinfoil for a remaining 30 minutes to prevent the crust from over-browning. The quiche is done when a knife comes out clean.

RUTH'S PRO-TIP
This is a flexible recipe, so feel free to play around with it. I sometimes add in some bacon or tomatoes and basil to add variety. Or use any flavorful cheese of your choice!

LA VIE EN

The Ladies Luncheon

- **Celebration Chicken Salad**
- **Arugula, Bacon, Avocado and Pistachio Salad**
- **Simply Perfection Shortbread Bars**
- **Strawberry Rhubarb Crisp**
- **Rosé**

Celebration Chicken Salad

I fiddled with this recipe until I got it just where I like it. It's a great dish year-round and works especially well for wedding and baby showers. There is something innately lady-like about chicken salad. Sometimes, I spoon it into sliced croissants. Other times, I serve it wrapped in large tortillas or lavash or on a simple bed of lettuce.

Any way you choose, it's delightful.

4 cups poached chicken
1 cup mayonnaise
1 small onion, diced
1 cup celery, diced
2 cups red seedless grapes, sliced
½ teaspoon cinnamon
salt and pepper to taste

Step 1: Shred the chicken (or for a smoother texture, use a food processor).
Step 2: Mix the mayo, onion, celery, grapes, cinnamon, and salt and pepper together.
Step 3: Combine with the chicken until evenly mixed.

RUTH'S PRO-TIP 

This recipe can be altered slightly to make a yummy curried chicken salad. Simply subtract the onion, celery, and cinnamon and add one healthy tablespoon of curry powder (or more to taste). Finish with a few tablespoons of sliced, toasted almonds.

Arugula, Bacon, Avocado, and Pistachio Salad

The first time my cousin Chrishelle made me this, it surprised me. Never before had I thought of arugula, bacon, pistachios, and avocado together. Boy, was I in for the tastiest revelation! The creaminess of the avocado pairs perfectly with the saltiness of the bacon. Meanwhile, the pistachios, fresh arugula, and light vinaigrette are meant to be together for eternity. We serve it alongside grilled chicken or steak on warm nights when no one wants to be inside.

4 strips thick-sliced bacon, diced
2 cups red grapes, halved
1 bag of arugula
1 avocado, diced
¼ cup roasted salted pistachios

VINAIGRETTE
¼ cup rice vinegar
3 tablespoons olive oil
1 tablespoon minced shallots
1 teaspoon honey
1 teaspoon dijon mustard
salt and pepper to taste

Step 1: Combine the grapes and arugula in a large bowl.
Step 2: Mix vinaigrette ingredients together, pour over the grapes and arugula, and toss.
Step 3: Garnish with avocado, bacon, and pistachios.

Simply Perfection Shortbread Bars

There is always a round of cheers when I announce I'm making these shortbread bars.

They are a bit different than traditional shortbread... They're softer and less crumbly. I think they're best eaten fresh out of the oven (and with a piping hot cup of tea!). It's also fun to add a bit of food coloring to the icing on holidays to make your cookies or bars a bit more festive. They look great dressed up in pink on Valentine's Day!

¾ lb. butter
1 cup sugar
1 teaspoon pure vanilla extract
3½ cups all-purpose flour
⅛ teaspoon salt
1 cup powdered sugar
1½ tablespoons water

Step 1: Preheat the oven to 350°F and line a 9x9-inch pan with wax paper.
Step 2: Mix the butter, sugar, vanilla, flour, and salt together. (It will be thick.)
Step 3: Press the dough into the pan.
Step 4: Bake for 25-30 minutes until the edges begin to brown.
Step 5: Mix the powdered sugar with water and drizzle on top once the bars are cooled.
Step 6: Slice the bars.

RUTH'S PRO-TIP
You can also roll the dough out to roughly a half-inch thick and cut out cookies using a cookie cutter. Bake at 350°F until lightly browned on a cookie sheet lined with wax paper. Remember: thicker is better.

Summer Strawberry Rhubarb Crisp

A summer's night spent on the patio eating this delicious crisp? That's my idea of heaven! This dessert is a perfect mix of textures and flavors, a classic made all the more exciting with the addition of luscious fresh strawberries.

½ cup flour
¾ cup sugar
¼ cup rolled oats
¼ teaspoon kosher salt
5 tablespoons cold butter cut into small pieces
1½ lbs. diced strawberries
¾ lb. diced rhubarb
3 tablespoons cornstarch

Step 1: Preheat your oven to 400°F.
Step 2: Grease 6 ramekins with butter.
Step 3: Mix flour, ¼ cup of sugar, oats, and salt together in a large mixing bowl until crumbly.
Step 4: In a separate bowl, combine the cornstarch with the remaining sugar.
Step 5: Coat the strawberries and rhubarb with the cornstarch/sugar mixture.
Step 6: Evenly fill the ramekins with the fruit.
Step 7: Spoon the oat mixture well over the top of the ramekin (don't worry, it will cook down).
Step 8: Bake for 30-40 minutes.
Step 9: Allow to cool 10 minutes before serving plain or with your choice of ice cream or whipped cream.

**I chill my Rosé and dress it up with a pink raspberry or a dash of Framboise (raspberry liquor).*

Summer

With the coming of summer comes the coming of family, whether it's a shared vacation with some of the cousins or a full-on "everyone is invited" family reunion.

Gathering the whole family together takes effort. As our extended family has grown, the opportunity to enjoy a holiday with those we love has become more challenging. There are a lot of schedules to juggle to make it work. That said, with every reunion, our bond as a family grows stronger.

During these precious summer days, the games and songs and stories do not end. By the light of the fire, another child grows up knowing who they are: a member of our family. Surrounded by those who have loved them since they were born and have committed to helping them grow up confident and strong in who they are, the next generation is reminded of their purpose and value.

Farm-Fresh Pesto Sammies

These pesto sandwiches taste like a summer garden. In reality, they are assembled more than cooked... perfect for those days when it is too hot to cook in the kitchen.

Note: The fresher the basil and tomatoes, the better the sandwiches. A watery, mealy tomato will ruin the whole effect. If you don't have a summer garden, go to your local farmer's market and find the best produce you can, along with some freshly baked bread. Believe me, the quality of the ingredients can make or break this sandwich.

4 slices ciabatta bread or rolls
prepared pesto
fresh tomato
fresh mozzarella
fresh basil

Step 1: Drizzle olive oil on two slices of bread.
Step 2: Broil until toasted.
Step 3: Spread pesto on top of each slice.
Step 4: Cut mozzarella and place on the bread.
Step 5: Place back under the broiler on a lower rack (be sure and keep a close watch!).
Step 6: After the cheese has melted, remove the bread slices from the oven and top with sliced tomato and freshly chopped basil leaves.

French Dip Sammies

This recipe for my favorite sandwich, French Dip, is the product of years of passionate experimentation. The meat becomes very tender over the cooking process and fills the house with an incredible aroma. It's a good year-round meal for a hearty weekend lunch or weeknight supper. It's also perfect to have around for all the teenagers that descend on my house on any given night.

1 large onion (cut into large chunks)
3-4 lbs. beef top roast
1 teaspoon Worcestershire
½ cup dry white wine
1 package au jus (I use McCormick)
2 cups beef broth

*French rolls

Step 1: Throw all the ingredients into a Dutch oven (or a crock-pot) and cook on low for 9-10 hours, until the meat falls apart.

Step 2: Right before serving, slice some good white French rolls. Butter them and toast under the broiler (make sure not to burn).

Step 3: Remove meat and slice thinly. (The idea is for your meat to look shaved.)

Step 4: Layer meat onto your toasted rolls. Serve hot!

RUTH PRO-TIP

I like to place provolone or American cheese on top. It's your choice. Save some of the beef broth for dipping!

Ribs Done Right (p. 216); The Porch in Summer; Family BBQ; Rustic Summer Blueberry Tart (P. 227); Make-Your-Day Cornbread (P. 218); French Bread; Hanging out by the fire pit.

Ribs Done Right

Years ago, I had ribs at my dear friend Bekah's. Tightly covered and baked for hours before throwing them on the grill to caramelize the edges with a generous slather of BBQ sauce, the meat was literally falling off the bone.

Seriously, who doesn't love a great BBQ meal? Indoors, outdoors, all seasons, these ribs are amazing. What's more, they are surprisingly low maintenance, which makes them perfect for events where you have a hundred other things to do. I love to pile the ribs high on a platter and serve them with baked beans, coleslaw, cornbread, and a Caprese salad.

2 racks of baby back pork ribs
The best BBQ sauce you can find!

Step 1: Preheat oven to 300°F.
Step 2: Cover a sheet pan with tinfoil and place the ribs bone side up.
Step 3: Cover the ribs with tinfoil and pinch the top and bottom together so the ribs are wrapped tightly in the foil.
Step 4: Bake 3-4 hours until you can separate the ribs from one another.
Step 5: Brush with your favorite BBQ sauce.
Step 6: Place on a medium heat grill. (I use an extra long spatula to move them to the grill or else they will fall apart.)
Step 7: Brush with more sauce, flip after a few minutes, repeat, and add more sauce. The sauce should be caramelized.

RUTH'S PRO-TIP
Serve these ribs with warm moist napkins. They are a little messy, and your guests will thank you. Twenty minutes before serving, I take damp cloth napkins and roll them up, placing them on a baking tray in a warm oven until the ribs are ready to serve. Right before everyone digs in, I pass them out using metal tongs so I don't burn my fingers! (And because it makes my dining room feel like a rib restaurant in Tennessee...)

Cool Iced Tea for Warm Summer Nights

Fill an ice tray with water and place a berry, a slice of orange, or pineapple into each cube. Freeze until solid. For your tea, boil 2 cups of water. Remove from heat and steep 6 regular size tea bags of your choice for 15 minutes. Remove the tea bags and pour the steeped tea into a large pitcher. Once cooled, add 6 cups of cold water and mix. Serve over the ice cubes and garnish with sugar, lemon wedges, and mint sprigs.

Make-Your-Day Cornbread

I don't mind admitting I fancy myself a cornbread connoisseur. I like it a little sweet and very moist. You'll never have to eat dry, crumbly cornbread again after making this recipe. For added deliciousness, I melt half a stick of butter and drizzle it over the freshly baked bread. Serve with ribs, chili, or pulled pork. For my family and friends, a BBQ is not the same without it. I don't know where my friend Caroline found this recipe, but I'm so grateful she shared it.

4 cups Bisquick
1 cup cornmeal
1 cup sugar
2 tablespoons baking powder
2 cups milk
4 eggs
2 sticks melted butter, plus another ½ stick melted butter for drizzling over top.

Step 1: Preheat oven to 350°F.
Step 2: Thoroughly mix the Bisquick, cornmeal, sugar, and baking powder together.
Step 3: Add in the milk, eggs, and butter and stir to combine.
Step 4: Pour into a greased 9x13-inch baking pan.
Step 5: Bake for 40 minutes until golden brown.
Step 6: Drizzle remaining melted butter over top.

RUTH'S PRO-TIP
For added sweetness, mix honey into the drizzling butter.

Black Bean and Corn Salad

This South-of-the-Border inspired salad is filling and refreshing. It's great on its own or paired with a cheesy casserole or burgers. I love the kick of cilantro and the creaminess of the diced avocados.

1 can black beans
2 cups corn (thawed if from frozen)
½ cup red onion
1 cup grape tomatoes
½ cup fresh cilantro
¼ cup extra virgin olive oil
2 tablespoons seasoned sweet rice vinegar
2 avocados

Step 1: Rinse and drain the beans and pour into a large serving bowl and add corn.
Step 2: Dice and add red onion.
Step 3: Slice and add tomatoes.
Step 4: Mince and add cilantro.
Step 5: In a separate bowl, combine olive oil, vinegar, and salt and pepper to taste.
Step 6: Pour over the vegetables and stir to combine.
Step 7: Lastly, carefully chop avocados into 1-inch pieces and gently stir them in.

Strawberry Romaine Salad

If any salad deserves a round of applause, it's this one. Maybe it's the saltiness of the bacon combined with the sweetness of the strawberries. Maybe it's the crunch of the sunflower and poppy seeds. Perhaps it's because the creamy dressing complements the crisp Romaine lettuce perfectly. Whatever the "it" factor is, this salad has it. Thank you Cousin Lori for introducing me to this salad!

SALAD
1 head Romaine lettuce
¼ cup crumbled bacon
1 pint strawberries
½ cup sunflower seeds
½ cup chopped red onion

DRESSING
1 tablespoon poppy seeds
2 tablespoons vinegar
½ cup mayonnaise
¼ cup milk
¼ cup sugar

Step 1: Chop Romaine lettuce.
Step 2. Toss lettuce with crumbled bacon, strawberries, sunflower seeds, and red onion.
Step 3: In a bowl, combine poppy seeds, vinegar, mayonnaise, milk, and sugar.
Step 4: Pour dressing over the lettuce. Toss and enjoy!

Picnic Berry Pie

Is there anything sweeter than the sight of young children sitting in a field on a blanket in summer enjoying picnic fare? Of course, all picnics are better with pie. This one is the taste of sunshine, summer, and endless days of fun.

TOPPING
1½ sticks butter
½ cup sugar
½ teaspoon pure vanilla extract
1¾ cups all-purpose flour
⅛ teaspoon salt

Mix the butter, sugar, vanilla, flour, and salt together, forming a crumble.

PIE
1 pint fresh blueberries
2 pints fresh chopped strawberries
1 pint raspberries
¼ cup tapioca
1 tablespoon butter
½ cup sugar

"A Very English Crust," (P. 272)

Step 1: Preheat the oven to 350°F.
Step 2: Combine berries with sugar and tapioca.
Step 3: Dice butter into small cubes.
Step 4: Dot cubed butter over berries.
Step 5: Distribute crumble over pie.
Step 6: Bake 1 hour or until bubbly.
Step 7: Allow to cool before serving.

Rustic Summer Blueberry Tart

Tarts are synonymous with the warm weather months. This particular blueberry version is an elegant edition to a late summer BBQ. It's gorgeous while maintaining a rustic simplicity. And it really is a treat for all of your senses.

TART SHELL
1½ cups flour
3 tablespoons sugar
1½ tablespoons cider vinegar
1½ sticks of butter
a pinch of salt

FILLING
6 cups fresh blueberries (not too ripe)
¾ cups sugar
3 tablespoons flour
3 tablespoons butter to dot on top

PREPARE SHELL
Step 1: Preheat the oven to 400°F and grease a 10-inch tart pan.
Step 2: Pulse flour, salt, sugar, vinegar, and butter in a food processor until crumbly.
Step 3: Press dough evenly into the tart pan.

ASSEMBLE TART
Step 1: Toss 4 cups of blueberries with the sugar and flour.
Step 2: Fill the prepared shell with 4 cups of the blueberry filling.
Step 3: Dot the top with the butter.
Step 4: Bake for 1 hour.
Step 5: Allow to cool.
Step 6: Pour the remaining 2 cups of fresh blueberries on top of the baked tart.

*Blackberries, marionberries, or currants (or a mixture of all three) can be substituted for the blueberries.

Racing to the next moment means that we might very well miss the moment we are in. Remember, the last slow days of summer are for savoring.

Autumn

AUTUMN: As the leaves begin to turn and the children return to school, once more I am reminded of how quickly time passes and how important it is to wisely use the time we've been given.

Today more than ever, a million things vie for our attention. Work follows us home long after we've clocked out. We check emails at three in the morning. We answer calls at eight at night. The lines between the office and home can easily become blurred. Juggling kids, careers, and the never-ending to-do list necessary to keep dozens of plates spinning at once is overwhelming. A modern epidemic of busyness threatens to infect each one of us. If we are not careful, a decade or two will pass, and we won't know what happened to the time or what we actually did with it.

In between meetings and school drop-offs, between takeout Chinese, and days without seeing your spouse because life is crazy sometimes, how do we make our homes something more than just a place we sleep or microwave leftovers? How do we slow down the clock and enjoy the days God has given us on earth? AUTUMN, for me, is the season to find out.

MAKING TIME

"All we have to decide is what to do with the time that is given us."

J.R.R. Tolkien (*The Fellowship of the Ring*)

HOW DO WE CAPTURE TIME?

Believe it or not, the answer is not difficult, but it does take self-discipline. Some things will have to give. Intentional, daily decisions to give generously of our time and attention to our friends and family are vital to healthy, stable homes… the sort of homes kids want to come back to when they are adults and off on their own.

Take a good look at your schedule. Do you really need to be doing so much? Could you wake up an hour earlier (and go to bed an hour earlier) to spend more time with your kids before school?

Ask yourself what you can do to create order and stability for your family. Simple things like eating together around the table once a week can have a huge impact. The point here is to eat together without a screen stealing our attention away from what matters most: each other.

Are you distracted by your phone or the television? Maybe you need to turn the volume down for a while so you can concentrate on what your kids or spouse are saying. Though we love a good movie night, it is essential to spend quality time on a regular basis without any screens invited… Little adjustments, like choosing to listen or celebrate little victories, can be all it takes to remind your family how much you value them.

ANGELO'S
SOCCER
CORNER

Intentionality

- Have a weekly family game night.
- Read out loud together.
- Cook together.
- Ask intentional questions at dinner. We love using conversation starter books.
- Give lots of hugs.
- Show interest in one another.
- Always say "I love you."
- Spend some quiet time with the kids before school each morning.

*Our weekly family game nights are legendary. Even our teenagers prioritize making it home for game night and often bring their friends. It's a blast. While Rook is the family favorite, we probably have over forty games to choose from.

SIMPLE AUTUMN DINNERS

- Vodka Marinara
- Mama Morken's Stroganoff
- Crispy Chicken Cutlets
- My Kids' Favorite Chicken
- Hillside Farm Peanut Butter Pie

Vodka Marinara

My mother passed away not long after I got married. In her absence, a woman in my Bible study, lovingly dubbed "Aunt Kim," took me under her wing and taught me to cook (something my mother and I had never mastered). Every time we met together, Kim taught me a new recipe that we would write down in a blank leather recipe journal.

Aunt Kim filled a void when my mom died for both myself and my children. Everything she does is beautiful, and her joy and patience in the kitchen are things I will forever be grateful for. She taught me to be present with my guests, even while preparing a meal.

This marinara recipe is one of the first recipes Aunt Kim taught me. I remember her in her home, stirring the sauce, pouring glasses of wine, and chatting with her guests seamlessly. She wasn't nervous to have people in her kitchen and made room for life to happen in the midst of entertaining.

It is simple and classic, like many of the recipes I learned in her kitchen. I haven't changed it one iota since I originally wrote it down in the journal. Some things do not need updating. This vodka marinara is one of them.

2 tablespoons olive oil
3 tablespoons butter
1 small onion, chopped
1 clove minced garlic
1 (28 oz.) can Italian plum tomatoes, diced
2 tablespoons chopped fresh basil
⅛ teaspoon red pepper flakes
½ cup vodka
½ cup heavy whipping cream
5 tablespoons freshly grated parmesan
1 (12 oz.) package cooked fresh linguini, or pasta of choice

Step 1: Melt the olive oil and butter in a saucepan.
Step 2: Throw in the onion and sauté for 5 minutes until translucent.
Step 3: Add the garlic and continue cooking for 1 minute. *Be careful not to burn.
Step 4: Stir in the tomatoes, basil, red pepper, and vodka. Simmer for 15 minutes to cook the alcohol down.
Step 5: Add in the cream and simmer an additional 5 minutes. Sprinkle parmesan in.
Step 6: Toss sauce with hot pasta and garnish with extra basil.

RUTH'S PRO-TIP 
I like to pair this sauce with cheese ravioli for a complete meal.

Mama Morken's Stroganoff

My sweet mama didn't cook much. However, she did know how to make this mean Hamburger Stroganoff. This child-friendly favorite is considered one of our tastiest dinners by a couple of my kids. I like to serve it the classic German way over wide egg noodles. Grill some asparagus or corn for fun sides.

3 lbs. lean ground beef
4 tablespoons butter
4 tablespoons oil
2 cups chopped onion
1 (12 oz.) can mushrooms
2 cans beef broth
3 tablespoons flour
½ teaspoon caraway seeds
4 cups sour cream
dash of nutmeg
dash of Worcestershire

Step 1: In a large hot skillet, brown ground beef and then drain.
Step 2: Melt butter and oil in a pan.
Step 3: Sauté the onion and mushrooms.
Step 4: Remove the onion and mushrooms and set aside in a separate dish.
Step 5: In the same skillet, add the flour and cook until thickened. Mix in the caraway seeds, nutmeg, and Worcestershire.
Step 6: Pour in broth, bring to a boil, and reduce heat.
Step 7: Add the meat and cooked mushrooms and onions to the broth. Simmer for a few minutes to thicken.
Step 8: Cook egg noodles until tender. Add sour cream to the beef mixture just before serving.
Step 9: Drain your noodles and spoon the beef stroganoff generously on top.

*Garnish with some chopped flat-leaf Italian parsley if desired.

Crispy Chicken Cutlets

Some nights, your kids just need an extra bit of happy. You know, something to make them smile. These "Crispy Chicken Cutlets" never fail to bring that dinnertime joy to my house. This recipe makes me happy too because oven fried chicken is so easy to clean up, and it's a lighter alternative to its deep fried cousin.

6 chicken breasts
½ cup melted butter
1 clove garlic, crushed
4 teaspoons dijon mustard
2 teaspoons Worcestershire
1½ cups bread crumbs
1 cup grated parmesan
1 tablespoon fresh parsley

Step 1: Preheat the oven to 350°F.
Step 2: Mix melted butter, garlic, dijon mustard, and Worcestershire sauce together.
Step 3: In a separate bowl, combine the bread crumbs with parmesan and parsley.
Step 4: Dip each chicken breast in the wet mixture.
Step 5: Dredge coated chicken breasts in the bread crumbs.
Step 6: Place on a lined and greased baking sheet.
Step 7: Bake 40 minutes.

RUTH'S PRO-TIP 

I love to serve these cutlets with my "Vodka Marinara Sauce" over ravioli (P. 244).

My Kids' Favorite Chicken

These twice-browned, bacon-wrapped, herby-cheesy, stuffed, baked chicken breasts are truly out of this world. My kids ask for them on repeat. Once you try them, you'll understand why.

4 chicken breasts
1 package Boursin cheese
4 slices bacon
2 tablespoons butter
2 tablespoons olive oil

Step 1: Preheat the oven to 350°F.
Step 2: Make a horizontal slice through chicken breasts to ¼-inch of the ends, creating a pocket.
Step 3: Melt butter and olive oil in a hot skillet.
Step 4: Brown the chicken 2 minutes on each side and move to a separate plate.
Step 5: Once cool enough to handle, spoon Boursin cheese evenly into the pocket of each chicken breast.
Step 6: Individually wrap each breast with a slice of bacon and secure with a toothpick if necessary.
Step 7: Place breasts back into the hot skillet and brown on both sides until bacon is crisp.
Step 8: Once browned, immediately slide the skillet into the oven for 30 minutes.
Step 9: Allow to cool 10 minutes before serving.

Hillside Farm Peanut Butter Pie

Bob and I have a favorite restaurant where we spend many of our date-nights. Our favorite dessert there is the famous "Peanut Butter Pie." On a whim, I decided to create my own version and present a slice of mine and a slice from the restaurant side by side in a blind taste test to the family. It was unanimous. Mine was better. Try it for yourself. Odds are, you'll agree!

CRUST:
27 Oreos
5 tablespoons melted butter

Step 1: Crush the Oreos until they are fine crumbs. (I use a food processor.)
Step 2: Mix the Oreo crumbs with melted butter.
Step 3: Press the mixture into a pie pan.
Step 4: Bake for 10 minutes at 325°F.
Step 5: Remove and allow to cool.

FILLING:
1 cup creamy peanut butter (I use Jiff, but any brand will work.)
1 (8 oz.) package cream cheese, softened
½ teaspoon vanilla
1¼ cups powdered sugar
2 (8 oz.) tubs of Cool Whip, thawed

Step 1: Beat the peanut butter, cream cheese, vanilla, powdered sugar, and one tub of Cool Whip together.
Step 2: Pour into the cooled crust.
Step 3: Spread the remaining tub of Cool Whip on top of the filling.

Chill the pie for at least an hour before serving.

Starting the Day Right

Nearly every morning, my kids and I wake up with the dawn. For fifteen minutes, before the mad rush to school and work and life tumbles down on us, we savor the quietness of being together. A few words read from a devotional or any old book we've grown to love, some eggs and toast and coffee, a pause to ground ourselves before we set out to conquer the day. Moments like this are the true "breakfast of champions," fortifying us for what lies ahead and reminding us of what truly matters before a million lesser things vie for our attention as our world starts out on yet another journey around the sun.

Saturday Sour Cream Pancakes

My stove has two built-in skillets so I can feed an entire army at once. My kids (and company) love to sit behind the island, forks in hand, as I flip these pancakes onto waiting plates. One of my daughters loves to add chocolate chips to hers... who's actually counting calories on pancake day, anyhow? Not us!

There are certain things I'm very particular about (as you know!) and pancakes are one of them. The best ones are thick and fluffy, and you can never stop with just one. The smell of these 1996 Junior League-inspired beauties cooking on a Saturday morning will get even the latest of sleepers out of bed!

2½ cups all-purpose flour
1 tablespoon baking powder
2 teaspoons baking soda
1 teaspoon kosher salt
1 tablespoon sugar
3 eggs
2 cups buttermilk
1 cup sour cream
2 tablespoons melted butter

Step 1: Heat the griddle to a medium heat.
Step 2: Combine all ingredients. (The batter is meant to be lumpy!)
Step 3: Carefully, pour the batter onto the griddle, about a half cup at a time. Space each pancake out by an inch or two.
Step 4: As little bubbles rise to the surface of the pancakes, flip them. You want the pancakes to be golden brown.
Step 5: Serve with a generous pat of butter, powdered sugar, and the syrup of your choice.

RUTH'S PRO-TIP

Cook time depends on your preference! I prefer a bit of a doughy center, while one of my daughters likes them on the "definitely more done" side. They are delicious both ways.

Perfect Protein Pancakes

Not long ago, I was staying at a lovely Bed and Breakfast, and they served a version of these fabulous protein pancakes. With Bob working on the property and the kids going from one swim meet to another, extra protein is always a plus. Regardless of the nutritional value, they are decadent and delicious on their own. You can feel good about serving these to yourself and your kids on those days when you need a little extra gas in your tank.

1 cup full-fat cottage cheese
½ cup flour
4 eggs
6 tablespoons melted butter (plus more for greasing the skillet).

Step 1: Melt the butter and let cool.
Step 2: Mix all ingredients (including butter) with an immersion blender until smooth.
Step 3: Spoon out a ¼ cup of batter onto a hot buttered skillet (as many as you can fit and still flip easily).
Step 4: When little bubbles form on the top, carefully flip the pancakes and cook the other side until golden brown.

Serve with syrup of choice or powdered sugar. (I know, I know, it kind of ruins the "good for you" argument. You could always top with fresh fruit!)

Best Brioche French Toast

This French Toast is the pinnacle of French Toasts, the best of the best. I get my brioche from Trader Joe's, which is pre-sliced. This recipe is so fabulous that you'll think you are eating dessert. I promise your entire family will be singing your praises all day after enjoying this for breakfast.

1 loaf of sliced brioche
6 eggs
½ cup half-and-half
1 tablespoon pure vanilla

Step 1: Whisk together the eggs, half-and-half, and vanilla.
Step 2: Melt butter into a large skillet on medium heat.
Step 3: Dunk the brioche into the batter.
Step 4: Place the brioche slice into the skillet. Flip when side #1 is lightly browned. Remove from skillet when side #2 is lightly browned. Continue until all the slices are cooked and golden on both sides.

Dollop the final pile of toast with warm butter and a generous scattering of powdered sugar (or drizzle with syrup of your choice).

Morning Bars

For a yummy, on-the-go breakfast, try my "Morning Bars." Sweetened almost entirely with dried fruit, it's perfect for kids on their way to school and parents getting started on their day. These bars make you feel good while still tasting good!

2 cups mixed nuts (I use almonds, walnuts, and pistachios)
1½ cups puffed rice
1 cup dried fruit, chopped if the pieces are large
(I use dried figs, mulberries, and apricots)
½ cup unsweetened coconut flakes
3 to 4 tablespoons seeds (sunflower seeds, chia seeds, etc.)
¼ teaspoon salt
1½ teaspoons pure vanilla extract
½ cup brown rice syrup
¼ cup almond butter or peanut butter
2 tablespoons coconut sugar (optional)
2 tablespoons chocolate chips (optional)

Step 1: Preheat your oven to 325°F.
Step 2: Line and grease an 8x8-inch square pan. For easy removal, extend the parchment paper above the top edge of the pan on at least two sides.
Step 3: Mix together the nuts, puffed rice, dried fruit, seeds, and salt in a large mixing bowl.
Step 4: In a separate bowl, combine the brown rice syrup, nut butter, and vanilla. It might help to gently heat the syrup and nut butter.
Step 5: Combine wet and dry ingredients.
Step 6: Press the mixture into the prepared pan. (Oil your fingers to keep the mixture from sticking.)
Step 7: Bake for 15 minutes and then allow to cool in the pan for 30 minutes.
Step 8: Lift parchment paper out of the pan and onto a cooling rack for an additional 30 minutes. Once completely cool, cut into 10 bars.

Have-an-Avo-Toast

Oh, avocado toast, how we love thee. Simple yet delectable, there's no wondering why it's taken the world by storm. With just a few simple steps, you can have a hearty, tasty snack or meal at your fingertips. Perfect for mornings on the run or a lazy dinner on the couch.

1 slice whole-grain bread
half an avocado
Everything-but-the-Bagel spice blend

Step 1: Toast bread in the toaster or oven until golden brown.
Step 2: Slice avocado. Using a fork, smash half an avocado onto the toast.
Step 3: Sprinkle with Everything-but-the-Bagel spice blend.

Crunchy Coconut Granola

Crunchy. Sweet. Savory. I like to always have granola on hand. It's a great snack on its own while also being delicious topped on Greek yogurt or eaten as cereal. There's no going wrong with this healthy, tasty treat.

1 gallon rolled oats
1 cup sliced almonds
1 cup pumpkin seeds
1 cup pistachios
½ cup flaxseed
½ cup chia seeds
1 cup shredded coconut
2 sticks butter
1 cup brown sugar
2 tablespoons cinnamon
1 tablespoon salt
1 cup honey
½ cup maple syrup
½ cup orange juice
4 tablespoons vanilla
dash of nutmeg

Step 1: Preheat the oven to 275°F.
Step 2: In a large bowl, combine oats, nuts, coconut, brown sugar, cinnamon, nutmeg, and salt.
Step 3: Spread the oats and nuts combination onto a cookie sheet and toast in the oven for 30 minutes.
Step 4: Simmer the honey, syrup, butter, orange juice, and vanilla in a pot.
Step 5: Pour the oats and nuts back into the large bowl and combine with the wet ingredients, mixing well.
Step 6: Place mixture onto a lined cookie sheet.
Step 7: Bake for another hour, moving mixture around every 15 minutes.
Step 8: Once the granola is golden brown, remove from the oven.

RUTH'S PRO-TIP 

I like to add dried fruit to our granola for added flavor! My favorites are cranberries, cherries, and apricots. *Remember, add the fruit after baking to prevent it from burning.

My orchard consists of eight Honeycrisp apple trees, a gift from my cousins David and Chrishelle after we babysat their six kids for two weeks so David could race across America on his bike. The trees have grown tall and strong since we planted them, and their fruit is profoundly sweet. Of every space on Hillside, the orchard in autumn may be my favorite.

i'm so glad i live in a world where there are Octobers

-L. M. Montgomery

In 2018, an enormous storm swept through Hillside. One of my beloved apple trees was uprooted, and we found it lying pitifully on its side the next day. I had no idea what to do but water the exposed roots and wait until a tree expert could come and assess whether it could be saved. The tree doctor came, dug out the remaining roots, replanted it, and tied it to several posts for extra support.

For a year, we tended it, loved it, and prayed over it. The result? It bore a full harvest of apples along with the rest of the trees!

Like my fragile apple tree, sometimes we need extra support. Sometimes one of us needs to be replanted and held up. Sometimes we need each other more than other times.

Sitting together in front of the hearth, snuggled on the couch to watch a movie or read a book together, doing homework at the table side by side… Simple acts of togetherness mend hearts and strengthen love and compassion. It keeps "family drift" from seeping in.

Orchard Apple Pie

During apple season, I make apple pie at least once a week. In fact, this recipe might be one of my favorite things about having my own little orchard. It's a bit different than some apple pie recipes because it focuses completely on letting the fresh apples themselves shine without muddying their flavor with strong spices. That said, it's important to use the tastiest, most flavorful apples you can find. My cousin Lisa turned me on to this recipe.

2 batches "A Very English Crust" (P. 272)
½ cup salted butter
3 tablespoons flour
¼ cup water
½ cup sugar
½ cup brown sugar
8 Granny Smith apples, peeled, cored, and sliced

Step 1: Preheat the oven to 425°F.
Step 2: Melt the butter in a pan and then stir in flour to form a roux.
Step 3: Add in water and both sugars and then boil. Once it begins to boil, turn the heat off.
Step 4: Roll one batch of your prepared crust into a large disk, about a quarter-inch thick, and press into the bottom of your pie pan. Fill with sliced, peeled apples.
Step 5: Drizzle the sugar and butter over the apples.
Step 6: Roll out the crust (about a quarter-inch thick) and place it over the apple mix. Pinch the edges of both shells together.
Step 7: Bake for 15 minutes and then reduce the temperature to 350°F. Continue baking for another 40 minutes.

Serve warm with ice cream or whipped cream.

"Good apple pies are a considerable part of our domestic happiness." Jane Austen

A Very English Crust

MAKES ONE 9-INCH CRUST

Years ago, I became friends with an English woman named Gillian who happened to be one of the area's best caterers. Often, my best friend Heather and I would help her with events. Whenever we loved a particular dish, she graciously shared her secrets.

This is her pie-crust recipe, and it is the best crust I've ever had. Actually, I never tried another recipe after discovering it. This crust never fails to flake, is perfectly salty, and just sweet enough. Everyone knows the perfect pie begins with the perfect crust. You'll be on a pie-baker's winning streak with any filling if you use this recipe as the base.

1¼ cups all-purpose flour
½ teaspoon salt
1 tablespoon sugar
6 tablespoons chilled unsalted butter, cut into ¼-inch pieces
4 tablespoons chilled all-vegetable shortening (I use Crisco butter-flavor sticks)
3 tablespoons ice water (more if needed)

Step 1: Pulse all ingredients in a food processor. Add an extra tablespoon of ice water if your dough needs more moisture to hold together.
Step 2: Press into a ball and chill until ready to use. (Bring to room temperature before rolling.)

RUTH'S PRO-TIP

I know that pre-made pie crusts are readily available, and I am a big fan of simplicity and shortcuts. That said, when it comes to pie crust, I always opt for homemade. I make this in batches and freeze in balls. After thawing on the counter or in the fridge overnight, I roll the dough out, and presto, homemade crust that's faster than going to the store and buying a pre-made one.

Apple-Goodness Cake 

Each fall, we harvest hundreds of apples from our trees—maybe that's why I have so many apple recipes! But this cake sure is special. The combination of vanilla, butter, sugar, and apples is nothing short of divine. It gives you a little taste of autumn no matter what time of year it is.

¾ cup flour
¾ teaspoon baking powder
¼ teaspoon kosher salt
2 apples (any kind)
⅔ cup sugar
2 teaspoons vanilla
¼ cup melted butter
2 eggs

Step 1: Preheat oven to 350°F.
Step 2: Core apples and dice small.
Step 3: Mix all dry ingredients together.
Step 4: Beat eggs until they are frothy.
Step 5: Combine vanilla with the eggs.
Step 6: Melt butter and allow to cool.
Step 7: Mix the cooled butter with the sugar.
Step 8: Combine the butter-sugar combination with the egg mixture.
Step 9: Combine all ingredients (dry, wet, and apples).
Step 10: Pour batter into a greased 8x8-inch pan.
Step 11: Bake for 45 minutes or until a toothpick comes out clean.

Autumn Apple Crisp

There's nothing like baking a piping hot apple crisp on a cool fall night. It's an easy, casual dessert, perfect for the family after a long day at school and football practice. Serve with rich vanilla ice cream or whipped cream.

FILLING
5 lbs. Granny Smith apples
2 tablespoons fresh orange juice
½ cup sugar
2 teaspoons cinnamon
1 teaspoon ground nutmeg

TOPPING
2½ cups flour
¾ cup lt. brown sugar
¾ cup sugar
½ teaspoon kosher salt
1 cup rolled oats
3 sticks chilled butter, diced

Step 1: Preheat the oven to 350°F and butter a 9x13-inch baking dish.
Step 2: Peel, core, and cut the apples into bite-sized pieces.
Step 3: Add the apples to the juice, sugar, and spices. Pour into the baking dish.
Step 4: To make the topping, combine the flour, sugars, salt, oats, and cold butter in the bowl of an electric mixer fitted with a paddle attachment. Mix on low-speed until the mixture is crumbly. You can also do this with your hands.
Step 5: Sprinkle the topping evenly over the apples.
Step 6: Place the baking dish on a sheet pan and bake for an hour until the top is brown and the apples are soft. Best served warm with vanilla ice cream.

RUTH'S PRO-TIP 
This recipe also works great with peaches and raspberries! Just omit the sugar and spices in the fruit mixture and bake as directed.

SHUTTING DOWN YOUR GARDEN

LATE AUTUMN

As winter approaches, so does the need to put your garden to bed. Perennials like irises, begonias, clematis, and daylilies need to be pruned after the first frost. Pull dead annuals, harvest late fruit or vegetables, remove overgrowth, and clean your gardening tools. Taking these steps now prevents pests and rot from moving in and taking over.

This is also the time to prepare for next spring. Plant bulbs such as daffodils and tulips now, and they will be the first to greet you when spring arrives.

MULLED CIDER

Bring 2 quarts of apple cider or unfiltered apple juice, 2 cinnamon sticks, 1 piece of fresh ginger, 2 allspice berries, 2 cloves, and 1 thinly sliced orange to a gentle simmer. If only adults are present, add 1½ cups bourbon, brandy, or dark rum.

In the midst of the daily grind, it is important to remember what we are thankful for.

I am thankful for my family.

I am thankful for the ability to work and to play.

I am thankful for adventure.

I am thankful for rest.

I am thankful for books.

I am thankful for music.

I am thankful...

THANKSGIVING

Every Thanksgiving, we read Abraham Lincoln's proclamation out loud, reminding us of what we have to be thankful for and who we need to bless.

"I do therefore invite my fellow citizens in every part of the United States… to set apart and observe the last Thursday of November next, as a day of Thanksgiving and Praise to our beneficent Father who dwelleth in the Heavens. And I recommend to them that while offering up the ascriptions justly due to Him… they do also, with humble penitence for our national perverseness and disobedience, commend to His tender care all those who have become widows, orphans, mourners or sufferers in the lamentable civil strife in which we are unavoidably engaged, and fervently implore the interposition of the Almighty Hand to heal the wounds of the nation and to restore it as soon as may be consistent with Divine purposes to the full enjoyment of peace, harmony, tranquility and Union."

Abraham Lincoln, Thanksgiving Proclamation, 1863.

ORCHARD APPLE PIE (P. 270); THANKSGIVING IN THE BARN; COOKIES AND SHORTBREAD (P. 105 AND P. 203); KITCHEN GATHERING; BACK PORCH; OUTDOOR SETTING; THE SWING.

Thanksgiving Favorites

Showstopper Corn Pudding

This never fails to show up on my Thanksgiving table. Even when competing with the turkey, potatoes, and stuffing, this always winds up as my favorite dish on the table (probably because of the bacon!).

The "pudding" is really a sort of soufflé, so you can imagine what a show-stopper it is coming out of the oven. And like a soufflé, simply spoon it out to serve.

1 (8 oz.) package corn muffin mix
1 (14 oz.) can whole kernel corn, drained
1 (14 oz.) can cream-style corn
1 cup sour cream
2 eggs
½ cup melted butter
¾ cup shredded cheddar cheese
10 slices crispy cooked bacon, crumbled

Step 1: Preheat the oven to 350°F.
Step 2: Thoroughly grease a 9x9-inch baking pan with nonstick spray.
Step 3: Combine the muffin mix with the whole kernel corn, cream-style corn, sour cream, eggs, and butter.
Step 4: Pour into the prepared pan and sprinkle the cheese and bacon on top.
Step 5: Bake for 50 minutes until golden brown on top and the center is set.

Dreamy, Creamy Potato Casserole

In my mind, the perfect potato casserole is creamy, just salty enough, cheesy, has the crunchiest of crunchy baked toppings, and comes together with minimal effort.

Aunt Kim's "Dreamy, Creamy Potato Casserole" meets all of my expectations and has stood the test of time. The best part is you don't have to peel one single potato. Serve alongside a juicy steak or as a holiday side. Once you try it, you'll never go back to plain-Jane mashed potatoes again.

2 lbs. frozen hash browns with peppers
½ cup melted butter (plus more for greasing the dish)
1 teaspoon salt
1 can cream of chicken soup
2 cups grated cheddar
½ cup onion, chopped
2 cups sour cream
2 cups crushed corn flakes

Step 1: Preheat the oven to 350°F.
Step 2: Thoroughly butter a 9x13-inch baking dish.
Step 3: Mix together the hash browns, salt, soup, cheese, onion, and sour cream. Spoon into the prepared dish.
Step 4: Combine the corn flakes with the melted butter and sprinkle the mixture over the top of the potatoes evenly.
Step 5: Bake for 45 minutes until golden brown.

"Praise God From Whom All Blessings Flow"

A GOOD HOSTESS MAKES MEMORIES OUT OF MISTAKES

One Thanksgiving, we cooked three turkeys and a ham for our 43 guests. Not one of the turkeys cooked in time, not even the one we deep fried! In the end, we stuck with the ham… Sometimes you just have to "go with it." We call that Thanksgiving, "43 People and a Ham," and we're still laughing about it.

Winter is a season unlike any other when it comes to feeling at home. In the words of Jane Austen, "There is nothing like staying at home for real comfort."

I THINK it has something to do with the cold and the snow. I want to stay inside by my fireplace, wrapped up in a flannel blanket, safe and secure with a good book, completely protected from the elements, with no need to perform or jostle my way through a crowd.

There is something about the cold weather that gives us permission to rest, go slow, and prepare for the new year ahead... in between the hustle and bustle of holiday parties and clearing mounds of snow!

Winter

HILLSIDE
FARM

Christmas at Hillside

A HOLIDAY DINNER MENU

Hillside Farm's Fillet

Foolproof Roasted Asparagus

Crème Brûlée

Ultra-Rich Hot Chocolate

Hillside Farm's Fillet

Every now and then, I love to surprise my family with a fancy, special meal! This fillet is incredibly simple to make but tastes straight out of a five-star steak house.

Leftovers are never a guarantee with this recipe, but if you do have some, slice the fillet thin and serve on good French bread for an "out of this world" steak sandwich.

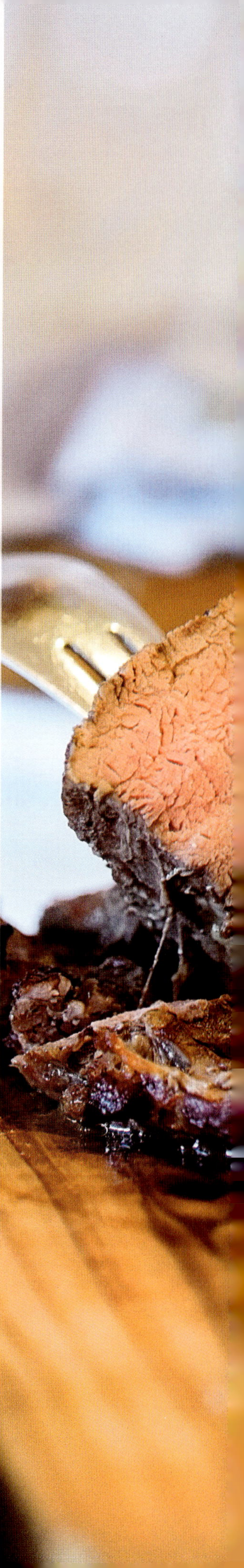

1 whole fillet of beef (4 to 5 lbs.), trimmed and tied
4 tablespoons salted butter at room temperature
1 tablespoon kosher salt
1½ tablespoons coarsely ground black pepper

Step 1: Place the fillet on your counter until it reaches room temperature and preheat the oven to 500°F.
Step 2: Place the fillet on a baking sheet and pat the outside dry with a paper towel. (I tie up the narrow end of the fillet with twine.)
Step 3: Spread on the butter. (I like to use my hands for this step!)
Step 4: Sprinkle evenly with salt and pepper.
Step 5: Roast in the oven for exactly 25 minutes for medium-rare or 30 minutes for medium.
Step 6: Remove the beef from the oven, place on grill on medium-high heat for one to two minutes on each side. Cover it tightly with Aluminum foil, and allow it to rest at room temperature for 20 minutes before slicing.

*Remember to cut against the grain of the meat. It keeps the meat juices inside rather than running out onto your cutting board.

RUTH'S PRO-TIP
I love to add even more richness, so I pour a quarter cup of melted butter on top of the beef before slicing.

Foolproof Roasted Asparagus

Asparagus is one of our favorite vegetables. In my opinion, it tastes good with almost any main course. My hubby loves it too, so this recipe is a definite go-To for us. The key is to not overcook the asparagus. Take it out of the oven while it is still tender and a little bit crisp. Serve with "Hillside Farm's Fillet" (P. 292).

2 lbs. fresh asparagus (break off the thick ends of the asparagus)
good quality olive oil for drizzling
½ teaspoon kosher salt
freshly ground black pepper, to taste
¾ cup shaved fresh parmesan
the juice of half a fresh lemon

Step 1: Preheat the oven to 400°F.
Step 2: Place a single layer of asparagus on a baking sheet and drizzle with olive oil.
Step 3: Sprinkle with salt and pepper.
Step 4: Roast for 15 minutes.
Step 5: Top with shaved parmesan and lemon juice.

RUTH'S PRO-TIP

This recipe also works great with Brussel sprouts. I love to add a little sweet chili sauce and crispy bacon on top after they come out of the oven. So tasty!

Crème Brûlée for Four

In English, "crème brûlée" means "burnt cream." In reality, you don't burn the cream at all. That said, you do caramelize a layer of sugar on top of perfectly baked and chilled vanilla custard. I've never met anyone who doesn't like crème brûlée. This version is one of the first recipes Aunt Kim taught me. I love to serve this in individual ramekins for dinner parties. It makes the simplest of meals a little bit fancy.

2 cups heavy whipping cream
5 egg yolks
½ cup sugar
1 tablespoon vanilla
½ cup lt. brown sugar

Step 1: Preheat the oven to 275°F.
Step 2: Whisk cream, yolks, sugar, and vanilla together. Pour evenly into four large ramekins.
Step 3: Fill a roasting pan with a half-inch of water. Carefully place the ramekins into the roasting pan "bath."
Step 4: Bake between 50 minutes and 65 minutes. The custard is cooked when a knife poked into one of the brûlées comes out clean. You don't want to over-bake it. A little jiggle is fine.
Step 5: Remove from the oven. Once cool enough to handle, transfer the ramekins onto a baking sheet and into the fridge until chilled and set.
Step 6: About a half-hour before serving, remove the tray from the fridge and evenly sprinkle about 1½ tablespoons of brown sugar on top of each brûlée.
Step 7: Place the tray of ramekins into the freezer for a half-hour. This helps keep the custard cool when you brûlée the sugar. No one likes a warm crème brûlée!
Step 8: Preheat the oven to broil and broil the brûlée until the sugar on top caramelizes. Of course, you can also use your kitchen blow torch... or a real one as Bob did once (with caution!).

Garnish with fresh berries.

Ultra-Rich Hot Chocolate

Follow the directions for your favorite hot chocolate mix but replace the water or milk with steaming hot heavy whipping cream. Top with assorted sizes of marshmallows. And if you are feeling extra celebratory, add a shot of Kahlua.

The Spring House

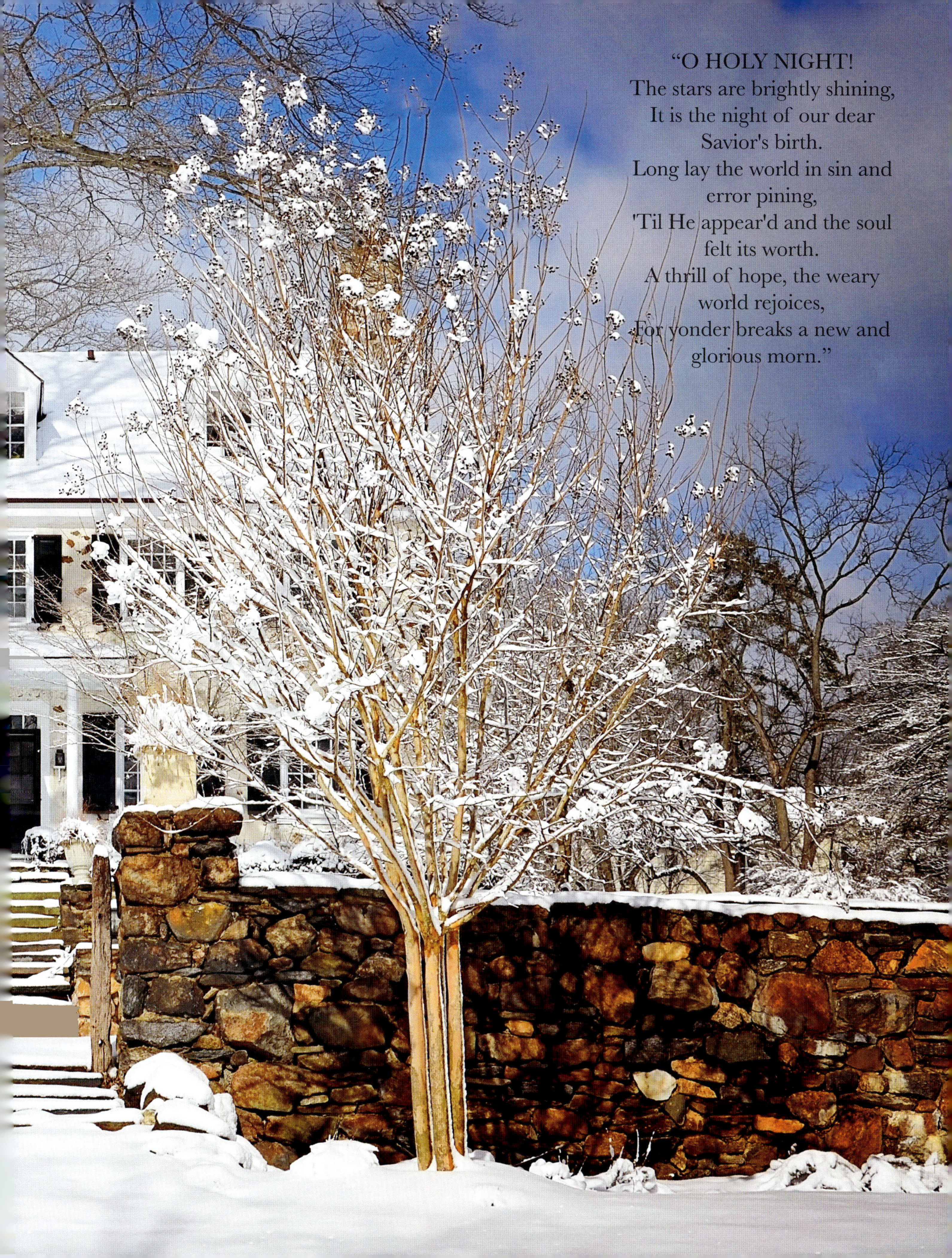
"O HOLY NIGHT!
The stars are brightly shining,
It is the night of our dear
Savior's birth.
Long lay the world in sin and
error pining,
'Til He appear'd and the soul
felt its worth.
A thrill of hope, the weary
world rejoices,
For yonder breaks a new and
glorious morn."

Christmas with the McKeaneys

THE CHRISTMAS DOORS

About a week or two before Christmas, I "wrap" the doors of the dining room to look like two enormous presents. From this day until Christmas, no one but Bob and I may enter the room. Behind its doors, we wrap presents and create other surprises for the kids. You can't imagine how much they love seeing those wrapped doors and feeling the anticipation of what Bob and I are preparing for them.

ON THE NIGHT BEFORE CHRISTMAS

Every Christmas Eve, we make about 400 sweet rolls to give away. It's a family affair. All seven of us (Bob, me, and the kids) create an assembly line to roll the dough, spread the filling, and fill seemingly endless tins with breakfast sweetness. I wish I could describe how delectable the kitchen smells on "sweet rolls day."

When all the preparations are finished, one of my daughters prints off the directions to tell each recipient how to let the rolls rise overnight, when to add the cream, and how long they should bake.

We wrap the rolls carefully, secure the directions on the top with a bright red bow, and load them up in the car. Half the fun is belting out carols as we deliver each Christmas surprise.

After the last sweet roll is delivered, we stop by our favorite Chinese neighborhood restaurant and order takeout. We dine on Moo Goo Gai Pan, Egg Drop Soup, and fried dumplings by candlelight on my best china. Christmas Eve wouldn't be Christmas Eve without Chinese food.

As soon as the meal is over, Bob and I lock eyes and count to three. The kids take off to the tree in the den on a crazy hunt to find the "pickle ornament."

THE PICKLE ORNAMENT

Whoever finds the pickle ornament on the tree has the honor of opening the first "Christmas box." The Christmas box contains the new things for the year—the new game, new ornament, new puzzle, and most importantly, the new book we will read together.

Everyone fetches their sleeping bags, including Bob and me. In front of the fire in the living room, we spread out in front of the tree and settle in to watch *White Christmas.* Cozy together, we fall asleep, all seven of us, by the light of the fire.

CHRISTMAS MORNING

In the morning, the kids wake us up with coffee and the fire roaring cheerfully. I slip the last tray of sweet rolls (reserved for us!) into the oven. After an enormous brunch, Bob reads the Christmas story, and we take turns opening presents, but only after they've found the ceramic baby Jesus that Bob and I have hidden while no one was watching.

But the sweetest gift of all is the time we spend together. Every single Christmas is a gift, and I value it more than any gift I've ever given or received.

Memory-Making Almond Roca

Each December, I gather Bob and my kids in the kitchen, and we make more than a dozen trays of our version of an old family recipe to give away as Christmas gifts. The night is always filled with laughter and excitement as we embark on one of our favorite holiday traditions. (I think it is especially fun because it includes so much butter and chocolate.)

By now, we have it down to a science and are down to 15 minutes a pan. That is a record! It's not only a fun and yummy memory to make, but it's always a big hit with our friends!

2 cups sugar
½ cup water
2 tablespoons lt. Karo syrup
1 lb. butter
2 cups slivered white almonds
1 lb. very good milk chocolate (chopped)
1 cup chopped walnuts

Step 1: Thoroughly grease a cookie sheet.
Step 2: Melt the chocolate in the microwave, stirring every thirty seconds or so to avoid it burning. Or melt on the stove over a double-boiler, stirring constantly.
Step 3: Combine the sugar, water, Karo syrup, butter, and slivered white almonds in a heavy stock pan on high heat.
Step 4: Stir constantly. When the mixture reaches the hard crack stage (between 300°F and 310°F), the almonds will look very toasted.
Step 5: Pour the sugar mixture evenly onto the cookie sheet.
Step 6: Immediately drizzle melted chocolate over the top until completely covered.
Step 7: Sprinkle the walnuts over the chocolate while it is still setting.
Step 8: Allow the chocolate to fully set. (You can speed the process up by sticking it in the fridge for an hour or so.)
Step 9: Break into large pieces. Enjoy!

Aunt Gladys' Sweet Rolls

My Great Aunt Gladys was one of the most amazing women I've ever known. She also knew how to bake like nobody's business. (In fact, Ronald Reagan asked her to be his personal cook at the White House when he won his first election after tasting her food on the campaign trail. She politely declined, but was very flattered nevertheless.)

Beyond her genius in the kitchen, Aunt Gladys had a giving, generous spirit. You could frequently find her at the local prison, dropping off baked goods for the inmates. Each night, she prayed for every family member by name, and that included her grandchildren and great-grandchildren.

Aunt Gladys made these rolls for every family celebration for as long as I can remember. My parents continued the tradition, and Bob and I have carried it on with our kids and make them for every birthday and holiday.

If you have little ones around, this recipe is a perfect family activity. Have one child dip the dough in water, another roll the dough in the cinnamon-sugar, etc. Growing up, my father was in charge of the sweet-roll line, telling all six kids what to do. These days, I'm the "Sweet Roll Factory" job delegator.

This version is my own iteration of her beloved classic.

1 thawed bag of 24 frozen yeast rolls
3 tablespoons cinnamon + 2 cups sugar, mixed together
1 cup heavy whipping cream, minus 2 tablespoons
1 stick melted butter
¾ cup lt. brown sugar
a bowl of water

Step 1: Preheat the oven to 350°F.
Step 2: Pour melted butter into a 9x13-inch pan and sprinkle the brown sugar evenly over the top.
Step 3: Dip each roll in water and roll in the cinnamon-sugar mixture.
Step 4: Stretch and tie each roll into a knot.
Step 5: Evenly place each roll into the pan.
Step 6: Cover the pan with tin foil and allow to rise overnight on your counter.
Step 7: Before baking, pour the heavy whipping cream over the risen rolls.
Step 8: Bake for 20 minutes, covered with foil. Remove the foil and bake an additional 10 minutes.
Step 9: Place a plate on top of the pan and flip the sweet rolls onto the plate.

THE NEW YEAR

A new year hints that the cycle is about to begin once more. Of course, no spring, summer, autumn, or winter is ever exactly the same. There will be new challenges. The kids will be a little taller. Bob and I will be a little older (and hopefully wiser!).

New Year's is one of the holidays that feels free and easy to me. Every year, we go to my cousin's home to celebrate. He spends weeks preparing an escape room, and together, we count down the hours to the new year trying to solve puzzles and riddles.

When the clock strikes midnight and fireworks sound out all over the city, no matter what the past year may have held, we made it through, together. And we trust that God will bring us through the following year, with all its unknowns, with peace and joy.

WINTER SOUPS

- I "Heart" Chicken and Wild Rice Soup
- Aunt Kim's Corn and Cheddar Chowder
- "This One's for Bob" Baked Potato Soup
- Chicken and Barley Soup
- Butternut Squash Soup

I "Heart" Chicken and Wild Rice Soup

One afternoon, while on a family vacation in Switzerland, Bob and I found ourselves in the courtyard of the most romantic restaurant, eating soup out of adorable bowls topped with crunchy pastries that were cut into charming hearts. (If you're curious, the kids were out on a paragliding expedition, and back then, I didn't do heights.) Ever since that trip, a shaped pastry graces the top of my "go to" winter soup, "Chicken and Wild Rice." Whenever I make it, it brings Bob and I right back to the Alps.

2 sticks butter
1 cup shredded carrots
¾ cup chopped celery
¾ cup chopped onion
6 cups shredded (cooked) chicken
8 cups chicken broth
2 chicken bouillon cubes
1 (6 oz.) package long grain and wild rice mix with herbs
8 oz. fresh mushrooms, sliced
½ cup flour
4 cups milk
frozen puff pastry

RUTH'S PRO-TIP

Brush pastries with an egg-white wash (a couple of whisked egg whites and a teaspoon of water) for extra shine before baking.

Step 1: Melt 1 stick of butter in a large Dutch oven.
Step 2: Add the celery, onions, and carrots and cook for approximately 5 minutes until vegetables are tender.
Step 3: Stir in the broth and bouillon cubes.
Step 4: Add the rice, seasoning mix, and chicken.
Step 5: Simmer for 40 minutes.
Step 6: In a separate skillet, melt the remaining stick of butter and then add the mushrooms.
Step 7: Mix in the flour and then the milk with the mushrooms. Cook until mixture is bubbly, stirring constantly.
Step 8: Add the mushroom mixture to the soup. Cook until thickened.
Step 9: Unfold thawed puff pastry (according to the instructions on pastry package) and cut into hearts using a cookie cutter. Bake according to instructions until golden. Place the hearts on top of your bowls of steaming soup.

Aunt Kim's Corn and Cheddar Chowder

If anything spells comfort food, it's Aunt Kim's chowder. Who doesn't have a love affair with bacon (which is probably why I love this particular chowder so much). It's a great weeknight soup and always a hit with the kids. Serve with buttered crusty bread on a cold winter night. It's even better the next day.

4 chicken breasts, cooked and chopped
8 bacon slices
1 onion, chopped
1 tablespoon butter
2 teaspoons cumin
3 tablespoons flour
4 cups chicken broth
½ cup heavy whipping cream
1 (10 oz.) package of frozen corn
½ pound of grated cheddar

Step 1: Pan fry your bacon and crumble once cooled, reserving rendered fat.
Step 2: Sauté onion in the leftover bacon grease and a tablespoon of butter.
Step 3: Whisk cumin and flour into the butter and cook for a few seconds (a roux).
Step 4: Whisk in chicken broth until the soup begins to thicken.
Step 5: Reduce heat to low. Add the corn, chicken, heavy whipping cream, and cheese. Heat through. Serve immediately.

"This One's for Bob" Baked Potato Soup

Twenty years ago, I went to a potluck, and someone brought "Baked Potato Soup." Little did I know how much my husband would like it. It's old-fashioned, creamy, filling, and requested year-round at my table. Odds are, you'll like it as much as Bob.

1 small can chicken broth (15 oz.)
⅔ cup butter (a stick and a third)
⅔ cup flour
7 cups milk
4 russet potatoes
4 green onions
12 slices of bacon, crumbled
2½ cups shredded cheddar cheese
1 cup sour cream
salt and pepper to taste

Step 1: Pierce potatoes with a fork and bake at 450°F until fork tender (about an hour). Peel and cube.
Step 2: Mix butter and flour together with a whisk in your soup pot over medium-low heat.
Step 3: Slowly add the chicken broth. Continue to stir.
Step 4: Add milk and whisk until the soup is thick.
Step 5: Add potatoes, green onions, crumbled bacon, cheese, sour cream, and salt and pepper.
Step 6: Simmer until you are ready to serve.

Chicken and Barley Soup

The great thing about my "Chicken and Barley Soup" is how comforting it is. Pairs well with a winter family night, snuggled on the couch.

8 cups chicken broth
8 cups cooked and shredded chicken breasts
1 cup butter
¾ cup flour
1 diced yellow onion
2 diced celery stalks
5 cups cooked barley
4 chicken bouillon cubes
1½ cups heavy whipping cream
12 slices bacon, cooked and crumbled
salt and pepper to taste

Step 1: In a large soup pot, melt ½ cup of butter.
Step 2: Sauté onions and celery until softened.
Step 3: Stir in the rest of the butter. When melted, stir in flour until a roux forms.
Step 4: Mix in heavy whipping cream until the roux thickens.
Step 5: Whisk in broth and bouillon cubes.
Step 6: Add chicken, barley, bacon, and salt and pepper and heat through.

Butternut Squash Soup

Butternut squash becomes sweet and creamy when cooked thoroughly. Its brilliant orange hue is a cheery sight on a cold day. Once the leaves have fallen, this "Butternut Squash Soup" becomes a staple on my dinner table. In the cooler months, I love to serve this as a weeknight dinner alongside a hearty kale salad. It's one of my favorites.

3 lbs. butternut squash, cubed
1 medium yellow onion, diced
2 stalks celery, diced
3 (14 oz.) cans chicken broth
2 tablespoons butter
½ cup heavy whipping cream
bacon, crumbled for garnish

Step 1: Combine the squash, onion, celery, and broth in a soup pot and bring to a boil.
Step 2: Once the squash is fork tender, use an immersion blender (carefully!) and blend until smooth and creamy.
Step 3: Add the butter to the soup. It creates a lovely velvety finish!
Step 4: Dish into bowls and drizzle with the cream. Sprinkle on a bit of bacon if you wish.

As winter turns to spring, another year begins. For us at Hillside, the new planting year begins in late February. Dead leaves are cleared from the beds as the last of the snow melts. I'll begin to plan what flowers to plant and when. I'll scrub down my gardening tools that have lain dormant all winter long in my garden shed. Aphids, slugs, and snails move in almost as quickly as the warming weather, feeding on thawing compost and plant roots. Now is the time to deal with them!

While it is still cool, I'll prune back trees and shrubs. It is easier this time of year when the wood structures of the plants are visible. It is a good idea to add a little fertilizer to the soil as you prune to help your plants heal quickly.

Once the weather is warm enough, I'll prepare the soil of the herb garden and the cutting garden by tilling it and adding compost or other nutrients where needed. Then come the bulbs and perennials and a healthy layer of mulch.
By March, we'll have an explosion of tulips. The quiet of winter will give way to the chirping of birds and kids running around the farm causing a joyful raucous. Fresh sweet air will sweep over the lawn, and the chickens will start to lay eggs. Life continues at home at Hillside, new life mixed with the old. And that is the meaning of home, isn't it? Life, and life in all its fullness.

In everyone's life, there comes a time when staying in is more appealing than going out. This seems especially true in the "in-between" weeks of winter and spring, when the flowers are just beginning to bloom and the soil is beginning to thaw.

Bob and I will, on occasion, pick up takeout and eat out on the barn porch or under the stars near the fire-pit. Or, if we are feeling energetic, we'll make something special just for the two of us. Afterwards, we'll settle in for one of our favorite movies or take a walk around the property. There is something about being at home that makes it easier to talk about the important things and fully enter into a place of rest.

DATE NIGHT AT HOME

Honeymooners' Pork Tenderloin

Our first year of marriage, Bob and I moved in with my Aunt Arlita for a month when we were in between houses. I learned this pork tenderloin recipe under her expert supervision, and we've never stopped making it. I serve it with a light green salad.

1 pork tenderloin
4 tablespoons honey
2 tablespoons brown sugar
2 tablespoons cider vinegar
1 tablespoon brown whole grain mustard

Step 1: Preheat the oven to 375°F.
Step 2: Mix honey, sugar, vinegar, and mustard. Coat the tenderloin with the mixture, and marinate in the fridge for one to two hours.
Step 3: Place the tenderloin in an oven-proof dish, along with any leftover marinade.
Step 4: Bake for 30 minutes, uncovered.

Creamy Parmesan Risotto

I learned this recipe in a cooking class Bob and I took for a date night, and over the years, it has become our own. I love to serve this risotto with my fillet and baked asparagus. It provides a subtle nuttiness (and cheesy goodness!) that's just a lot tastier than plain rice.

2 cups Arborio rice
5½ cups simmering chicken stock
1½ cups freshly grated parmesan cheese
¾ cup dry white wine
3 tablespoons butter
2 teaspoons kosher salt
1 teaspoon freshly ground black pepper

Step 1: Place the rice and 4 cups of the chicken stock into a pot and simmer until the liquid is absorbed.
Step 2: Add in the remaining chicken stock, parmesan, wine, butter, and salt and pepper. Stir vigorously for 2 to 3 minutes until the rice is thick and creamy. Serve hot.

Jane's Chocolate Lava Cake

Chocolate. Lava. Cake. Need I say more? If you've had it, you know why. If you haven't, buckle up for a life-changing moment. It's an easy crowd-pleaser and never gets old. My friend Jane gave it to me twenty years ago, and I still make it to this day.

2 eggs
1 cup sugar
½ cup flour
¼ teaspoon salt
1 stick butter (plus more for greasing pan)
2 heaping tablespoons cocoa
1 teaspoon vanilla

Step 1: Preheat the oven to 300°F.
Step 2: Grease a loaf pan.
Step 3: Beat the eggs, sugar, flour, and salt together.
Step 4: Stir cocoa into melted butter and add vanilla.
Step 5: Pour the cocoa mixture into the egg mixture and stir to combine.
Step 6: Pour the batter into the prepared pan and bake for about 35 minutes. When the middle is still pudding-y remove from the oven and serve warm with extra-creamy vanilla ice cream and berries.

*Note, do not over bake!

RUTH'S PRO-TIP

I love to cook individual desserts for dinner parties. I think it makes people feel extra-special and more cared for when you have prepared something especially for them.

To make personal chocolate lava cakes, pour the batter into individual ramekins (don't forget to butter them!) and bake until the centers are just set and top with vanilla ice cream.

No matter how wonderful and comfortable our homes are, they will never fully satisfy our longing for something more. That something more is a Heavenly home. A home where all fears are stilled, all needs are met, and loneliness is a distant memory.

In the words of C.S. Lewis, "The fact that our heart yearns for something Earth can't supply is proof that Heaven must be our home."

All of us "home-makers" can accomplish only so much through our efforts to fill a void only Heaven can truly fill. These efforts, however, are important. The ability to make others feel loved, welcome, and cared for during their journeys through life is one of the greatest gifts we can give.

As we part ways, know that you are BLESSED:

BLESSED to feel truly at home wherever you are,

BLESSED to make a home wherever you are, and

BLESSED to be a BLESSING wherever you are and whoever you are with.

Ruth 

Recipe List

Breakfast

Drinks

Salads

Sides and Starters

Sandwiches

Soups

Mains

Sweets

NOTES

Abraham Lincoln, Thanksgiving Proclamation 1863.
Lincoln, Abraham. "Thanksgiving Proclamation." Speech, Washington DC, October 3, 1863. The White House. Accessed July 29, 2020. https://obamawhitehouse.archives.gov/

"All we have to decide is what to do with the time that is given us." Tolkien, J.R.R. *The Fellowship of the Ring: Being the First Part of the Lord of the Rings*. New Tork: Del Rey, 2015.

"And the secret garden bloomed and bloomed and every morning revealed new miracles." Burnett, Frances Hodson. *The Secret Garden.* New York: HarperCollins, 1911.

"Children growing up in an atmosphere where beauty is considered an important part of daily life cannot help being inspired to develop their own original ideas in these areas, nor can they help being prepared to live aesthetically themselves. There is a 'togetherness' in sharing a prepared table that even very small children feel, although they cannot express it verbally." Schaeffer, Edith. *The Hidden Art of Homemaking.* Wheaton: Tyndale House Publishers, Inc., 1971.

"Good apple pies are a considerable part of our domestic happiness." Jane Austen "Famous Fictional Pies." *Huffington Post,* March 14, 2015. Accessed July 29, 2020. https://www.huffpost.com/entry/famous-fictional-pies_b_6865944

"Gardens are not made by singing, 'Oh how beautiful' and sitting in the shade.." Kiplin, Rudyard. "The Glory of the Garden." Bartleby.com. 1922. Accessed July 29, 2020. https://www.bartleby.com/364/413.html

"Home is the nicest word there is." *Little House on the Prairie.* "A Harvest of Friends." IMDb TV, 49:09. September 11, 1974. Accessed July 29, 2020. https://www.amazon.com/Little-House-Prairie-Pilot/dp/B00J8BZRF0/ref=sr_1_2?dchild=1&keywords=little+house+on+the+prairie&qid=1595967375&sr=8-2

"I'm so glad I live in a world where there are Octobers." Montgomery, L.M. Anne of Green Gables. New York: Grosset & Dunlap, 1908.

"If you have a garden and a library, you have everything you need." Cicero, Marcus Tullius. ""If you have a garden and a library, you have everything you need." Marcus Tullius Cicero."" Henrietta Public Library, May 16, 2013. Accessed July 29, 2020. https://www.hpl.org/news/if-you-have-garden-and-library-you-have-everything-you-need/

"O Holy Night." John Sullivan Dwight, based on the French text from Placide Cappeau's Cantique de Noel. Adolphe, Adam (translated by John Sullivan Dwight). *O Holy Night.* (Sudds, W.F., 1883). Accessed July 29, 2020. https://www.loc.gov/resource/sm1883.19142.0?st=gallery.

"Next to trying and winning, the best thing is trying and failing." Montgomery, Lucy Maud. *Anne of Green Gables.* New York: Grosset & Dunlap, 1908.

BIBLIOGRAPHY

Garrison, James B. *Stone Houses.* New York: Rizzoli, 2013.

Feinberg, Margaret. *Taste and See.* Grand Rapids: Zondervan, 2019.

Holy Bible: New American Standard Bible. 1995. LaHabra, CA: The Lockman Foundation.

McKay, Brett and Kate McKay. "Creating a Positive Family Culture: How and Why to Create a Family Mission Statement." Art of Manliness. August 21, 2013. Accessed July 29, 2020. https://www.artofmanliness.com/articles/creating-a-family-culture-how-and-why-to-create-a-family-mission-statement/

HfH